For my amazing wife Chris: Marrying you
in 1978 was the best decision of my life.

Contents

Acknowledgments

A ny book starts with one or more ideas that tend to roll around in your head for a while, percolate and then, one day, you realize that you may have the material for a book. For this book, the initial work that wound up in these pages was all done around collaborative innovation with three amazing people, Tim Brostrum from the Fieldstone Alliance, Fran Loosen, now with the Kellogg Foundation, and Jeff Nugent, from The Center for Leadership Innovation. Tim, Fran, Jeff, and I worked together for just more than 18 months, and our conversations and collaboration were one of the personal highlights of my career in nonprofits. You see the results of their inspiration throughout the book.

The next person I have to thank is Deborah Atkinson, Executive Director of Learning and Performance Excellence at NISH, a national nonprofit headquartered in Vienna, Virginia. Deborah runs the best national training program for nonprofits anywhere, and I've had the privilege of working with, and learning from, her for nearly 20 years. Deborah saw a presentation I did on collaborative innovation in Port of Spain, Trinidad, and asked me to flesh out a two-day training course that was about innovation in a rapid growth environment. As I thought through the pieces of that course one afternoon, I had my "Aha! There's a book in this material!" moment, and Deborah gets much of the credit for improving the material contained here.

I spent considerable time working with the three case organizations, whose chief executive officers (CEOs) and staff gave me great feedback and anecdotes about their experiences with decision making and organizational growth. All three are exemplary nonprofits, among the best the United States has, and I greatly appreciate all the time and energy they devoted to helping me. Particular thanks go to Mitch Tomlinson and the staff at Peckham Industries in Lansing, Michigan, "Mark" and staff at "Lakeview Christian Church," and Ray Bishop and his staff at Goodwill Industries of North Georgia. You all are an inspiration, both to me and to your communities.

Introduction

Chapter Thumbnail

Overview

Welcome.

I hope this finds your nonprofit stable, growing at a healthy pace, providing high-quality mission, and using best practices in management, human resources, technology, and finance. I also hope your board fully understands the mission and the staff, and that all of your organization's key stakeholders are in lockstep as to your mission priorities, values, and the best way forward.

I hope.

Unfortunately, if you are like most nonprofit staff or volunteers, when you read the paragraph above you thought, for all or part of it, "I wish."

So do I.

This book is designed to be a tool to get your organization closer to the nonprofit nirvana described above. In my 30 years staffing, leading, volunteering, consulting, and training nonprofits, I have seen many nonprofits that are in the place described above. It's hard to get there and harder to stay there. It requires constant management and board attention to mission, values, culture, communications, and the entire community of stakeholders. Even when you are doing everything on that list, it's easy to go off course.

1

I hold a private pilot's license and flew regularly for 25 years. I've also sailed all my life. It always intrigued me that the rule in both disciplines is the same: "Look away for *three seconds* and you're off course." Three seconds. Thus, constant attention to your desired direction is crucial. First, though, you've got to get yourself and your nonprofit on the best mission course to start with.

And that's really what this book is about. Helping you get the mission, values, culture, tools, and skills to get your nonprofit on the right path and keep it there. For some organizations this will require big decisions and major course corrections. For others, a tweak here and an improvement there and you'll nearly be on autopilot.

In the pages that follow, I'll show you how to become a Smart Steward of your nonprofit's resources, and how to develop and use a decision making framework that your board and staff can use to move your mission forward, as well as the work that needs to be in place before you build that framework. A common decision process that is fully understood by staff and board is a huge advantage to your mission maximization efforts.

We'll also discuss developing a culture of constant innovation, both in the why and the how, and I'll provide you with tools to solve the knottiest problems out there. We'll investigate ways to incorporate your mission and values in everything everyone does in your nonprofit every day.

The ultimate goal, of course, is better mission for the people you serve. Sometimes better mission comes from a small, tactical decision made right at the line of service. Sometimes it's a huge strategic policy choice made by the board of directors. But whether big or small, all your decisions should make your organization more mission capable in very specific ways we'll examine in the coming pages.

The examples, cases, and hands-on ideas should give you things to use right away as you read each chapter. In addition, I've provided discussion questions for you at the end of each chapter to allow you to apply what you've learned immediately in your organization.

I hope this book helps you, your board, and staff advance your mission. The people who depend on your nonprofit for service hope so too.

The Need for This Book

This book is written as the United States is beginning to (very) slowly come out of the Great Recession, and much has been written about the effects of the downturn on the nonprofit community; the impact on fundraising, the number of layoffs, the hundreds, even thousands, of nonprofits that have shut their doors. All of which is true.

What you don't hear about is the other side: That nonprofits continue to be formed in great numbers, and that many are growing rapidly. I work closely with a national nonprofit with more than 350 affiliate local 501(c)(3)s whose goal is to double their network in size in five years. That's an annual 15 percent growth rate compounded. As I write this, I am also serving on the board of Goodwill Industries International. Even in the teeth of the worst of the recession, most Goodwill local chapters grew, because of more shopping in their stores and also because of a need for their job-placement services.

Educational, health care, employment, and housing nonprofits have all grown rapidly in many communities. As have, and here's the key, the best nonprofits.

 FOR EXAMPLE: The Bank of America (BofA) Neighborhood Excellence Leadership Program has, for many years, awarded a $200,000 grant to two nonprofits annually in each of the 45 largest markets in the United States and United Kingdom where BofA operates. Selected by a jury of their peer nonprofits in each community, the chief executive officer (CEO) and one Emerging Leader attend a number of multi-day training sessions on leadership and moving their organization forward. The recipient groups are from all parts of the nonprofit spectrum, from housing organizations to Kipp Schools, to Boys and Girls Clubs.

As a result of the awards, 92 CEOs and 92 Emerging Leaders meet, network, and learn together for three days, and I'm fortunate to get to work with both groups for a half-day each year. Starting in 2008, at the very depths of the recession, I began to ask the groups about the recession and how it affected them, assuming that layoffs and program shrinkage would be common. They weren't. Perhaps 5 percent of the room raised their hands when asked if they were contemplating or had just completed layoffs. Same for program cuts.

Why were these organizations exempt from the toll of the recession? Because they were financially stable, could make good decisions quickly, and had a culture that was resilient based on their commitment to their mission. ∎

These organizations did well in the face of adversity because they had many of the characteristics I described above of nonprofit nirvana. And, trust me, they worked hard to get there. They come from all parts of the nonprofit universe. Some are heavily government funded, some get almost all their funds from contracts, others from donations. They are as varied as can be, but all are succeeding in a tough economic environment.

My point? While some nonprofits are struggling, others are considering growth. Both paths need good decision-making tools, and in both situations staff and board members need to understand the implications of growth, going to scale, or staying small. All of this will be covered in the chapters that follow.

Speaking of "going to scale" this is a trendy, trendy term right now in the foundation world and one, as you'll see later in the book, that I think is very dangerous. But "scale" is what funders seem to think that they want, so if you're going after funds with that expectation, the tools you'll find here will help you immensely.

Next, I think a book like this is needed as the much-anticipated change in leadership at the staff and board levels from Baby Boomers to GenX actually begins to take shape. A new generation of leadership needs decision tools that they can build a consensus around, and the following pages will show you how.

Finally, there's technology. You'll see that I repeatedly urge you to ask as many people as possible, on both a large and small scale, for input into your decisions, and then broadcast your intentions widely to increase input, interest, and to hold you accountable to the community you serve. Technology makes this so easy and so inexpensive that it would be bad stewardship not to use the resources available to you to move your mission forward. More on that later as well.

I hope you agree that the time is right for this book. Now, let's look at who the target audience is, and then how to get the most from the time you invest in reading.

Who This Book Is Written For

If you are a decision-maker in your nonprofit, this book is for you. If you're involved in long range planning, strategy setting, day-to-day operations, this book has value. If you're a CEO or a front-line supervisor, there's material here for you. If you are a governing volunteer or paid staff, the material in the following chapters can help you do your job better.

And here's the key: By the time you finish the book (particularly Chapter 7 on Innovation), you *should* have more people involved in decision making than you do now. More staff, more funders, more community members, more people you serve. Thus, while many organizations will have just their senior management read this book initially, I hope that most of those nonprofits urge their entire board, all supervisors, key volunteers, and funders to read all or part of the book as well.

Why? Because everyone in a nonprofit has to understand ways that they can be Smart Stewards. The primary job of a steward is to get as much mission out the door every day as possible using all the resources that are available. Some of those resources are your mission, your values, your reputation, sure. But others are those wonderful staff, board, non-governing volunteers, and community members, all of whom are eager to help you do more and better mission.

If you are in conflict over how to proceed, involving all those groups is a detriment to mission. If you're in sync (and this book will show you how to get there) you can turbo charge your mission.

Finally, if you're a senior manager or CEO, you have to remember that you only have 24 hours in every day: You can't make every decision, set every strategy, solve every problem, come up with every innovation by yourself. A Smart Steward grows and encourages other Smart Stewards, and gives them the freedom to innovate, decide, take action and move forward, within the agreed-upon decision framework.

Because your organization can't have too many Smart Stewards around.

The Benefits of Reading This Book

I always make the assumption in writing my books that readers have jobs, lives, families, friends, hobbies, and community commitments as well as the need to actually sleep every so often. Thus I view your time with this book as an investment, one that should pay off in more mission for the people your organization serves. But, I need to convince you to continue to read, so here is my list of benefits that should accrue to you (and through you to your organization) from reading the pages that follow.

When you are through with this book, you will:

☐ Understand why your mission is your most valuable asset
☐ Be clear on why posting an organizational profit is good for your mission
☐ Have a clear understanding of why your organizational values are the foundation of your nonprofit's culture
☐ Be able to explain, adapt, and use the Smart Stewardship Decision Tree, and develop a similar decision matrix for your nonprofit
☐ Have identified your nonprofit's core competencies, as well as your core adequacies
☐ Be able to calculate the cost of growth (both large and small) each fiscal year
☐ Understand the risk to quality in a fast growth situation and methods to avoid a quality lapse
☐ Be comfortable with including more people in decision making and overall innovation in your nonprofit

☐ Know the main methods of going to scale, as well as the risks inherent in that strategic decision
☐ Understand the ways to evaluate growing versus staying small
☐ Be able to sort out strategic versus tactical decisions in a crisis
☐ Be better able to lead your organization in tough times

Read the list carefully. If that set of outcomes works for you, if you believe, as I do, that having those benefits will help your organization do more and better mission, read on. If not, I would urge you to not invest your time with what follows.

A Preview of the Book

In a moment we'll take the opportunity to preview the chapters that follow, but I want to make a few suggestions about how to get the most of the material in those chapters.

First, I suggest that you read the book as a team. Don't just go off and read what follows by yourself. Use it as a way of developing discussions and debates about the path your nonprofit should follow. Put together a team of people and either get them all copies of the book or pass this copy around. Read a chapter at a time, and then use the discussion questions at the end of the chapter to see what ideas I've laid out that you like, which you can implement immediately, which should be put aside for later action, and which you don't think fit into your nonprofit. Trust me. You'll get much, much more out of the material in this book if you read it as a team.

Second, I suggest that you read the book in the order it's written. That said, if you are particularly interested in the material on, say innovation or going to scale, *please* don't jump to that before you read Chapters 2, 3 and 4, as they form the philosophical basis for the materials in the later chapters. I know you're eager to get started, but starting at the beginning will be beneficial to you.

Finally, don't forget to review the Tools and Resources in the Appendix. They can supplement your learning and help you in specific situations you may face.

With those cautions and suggestions, let's examine the book chapter by chapter.

Chapter 1: Introduction

This is the chapter you are reading now. It includes a discussion on why the book is needed, who it is written for, some specific benefits you'll garner from reading the book, and a thumbnail review of each chapter.

Chapter 2: The Keys to Smart Stewardship for Your Nonprofit

This chapter lays the philosophical groundwork for everything that follows. You'll read about why every strategy and decision should start and end with mission, how mission, money, and innovation interact to produce Smart Stewardship, why profit is essential for good mission, and how to engage more people in your decision making. As I said earlier, if you choose only to read parts of the book, make sure you start here.

Chapter 3: The Smart Stewardship Decision Tree

Based on my work with very successful nonprofits, I've developed a Smart Stewardship Decision Tree and this chapter will allow us to look at it step by step and put it into use immediately for your nonprofit. You'll be seeing the decision tree at the beginning of each subsequent chapter, so make sure you read about it here first.

Chapter 4: Mission and Values

This chapter will show you some new ways to look at what is the foundation of your nonprofit: your mission and values. You can't be a Smart Steward if you don't always start and end with mission. The mission is the why of your nonprofit; the reason it exists. Your values are the how of your organization; they are the rules of the road as you provide mission to the people and community who depend on you. This chapter shows you how to get more out of both your mission and your values.

Chapter 5: Understanding Capability and Capacity

In the nonprofit world, we've done so much for so long with so little we sometimes think we can do everything with nothing. The truth, of course, is that we can't. And, Smart Stewardship requires that we do more of what we're really good at, and only grow when we have the capacity to do so. This chapter will focus on figuring out what your nonprofit's core competencies are, and how much capacity you should have before you embark on providing new programs or areas of service.

Chapter 6: Understanding the True Cost of Growth

Growth is good. Always. Grow or die. That's the common and very dangerous mantra of businesses, funders, and, often, our own boards. This chapter will help you better understand the cost of growth in terms of cash and quality, the impact of growth on management and line staff, as well as the people you serve. The truth is that growth is often a good thing in nonprofits, but not always, and this chapter will help you figure out the difference.

Chapter 7: Innovation as the Norm

All the easy problems have been solved. The tough ones, in large part, have been left to nonprofits to solve. No nonprofit can succeed without regular innovation at the point of mission provision. This chapter will show you how to "put more neurons on the problem" in ways you might never have considered, and how to bake constant innovation into your organizational culture.

Chapter 8: Going to Scale

Being able to "scale your idea" is one of the trendiest phrases in philanthropy. It's also one of the most dangerous. This chapter will give you tools to examine your ability to grow rapidly, to decide how much time and treasure you want to invest, and show you some different models for scaling your operations. I will also caution you (again) about the perils of rapid growth.

Chapter 9: Smart Stewardship in Difficult Times

This chapter looks at leadership and decision making in the teeth of a storm. Are the processes the same? How do you know how big a crisis you are facing? How do you keep your people's eyes on the prize? This chapter will show you how.

Chapter 10: Final Words

This brief chapter is intended to send you on your way motivated and ready to improve your nonprofit's mission-effectiveness, while at the same time giving you a few more hands-on ways to implement the material you've just read.

Appendix: Tools and Resources

In this chapter you will find recommended tools, books, papers, and Web-based resources to help you dig deeper into the issues covered in the book. I try to limit the amount of material I recommend to only the top few in each category, in order to avoid readers looking at the list and being overwhelmed. Thus, the materials and resources here have been carefully vetted.

Our Three Case Organizations

You'll see lots of examples of real world organizations throughout the book, but three cases will show up repeatedly. I selected them because they are great examples of organizations that have developed internal mission, values, and decision processes that have benefited the organization and the people that they serve. They are diverse in size, mission focus, and source of income. All have grown significantly in the past decade, and each has taken a different path in scaling, innovation, and community involvement. Here's a thumbnail of each organization.

Goodwill Industries of North Georgia (GING)

GING serves the northern part of Georgia, including the Atlanta metropolitan area, with services to help people become and stay employed. With a history dating back to 1925, GING has deep roots in the community. Like all Goodwills, the foundation of GING's business model is retail sale of donated goods, currently carried out in 36 stores across their service territory. Profits from these stores fund other employment programs.

One key to their success has been their executive team, led by CEO Ray Bishop. The entire team has been together for more than a decade. See more about GING at their web site: www.ging.org

> **Growth over past decade:** In 2001, GING posted $20.8 million in revenue. By 2011, they had grown to just more than $100 million of income. Their strategic plan calls for 2014 revenue to top $134 million.
> **Scaling Choice:** Opening more donation centers and thrift stores throughout its assigned territory. Note: Goodwills must limit their geographic growth to the territory assigned by Goodwill Industries International.

Lakeview Christian Church (Lakeview)

Lakeview is an independent Christian church in a mid-sized city in the Central Time Zone of the United States. (In Lakeview's case, their real name has been changed, as has the name of their senior pastor.) In 2000, a new senior pastor, Mark, was hired to succeed a retiring and very popular pastor who had been in place for more than 25 years, and who had both grown the church and had overseen the construction of a large new sanctuary and church school. Mark was in his mid-thirties when he became senior minister, and faced a number of challenges, including how to continue to grow the church in a community where population growth had been stagnant for 20 years.

Growth over the past decade: The growth metric Lakeview uses is weekly attendance. In 2000, this number was 1,500 and in 2010 it averaged 2,250 per week. A fourth Sunday service was recently added.

Scaling Choice: Organic growth on-site and planting churches in other locations.

Peckham Industries (Peckham)

Peckham Industries, based in Lansing, Michigan, helps people with disabilities and other significant employment challenges find meaningful jobs, either at Peckham or in the community. Led by CEO Mitch Tomlinson, Peckham has grown rapidly in Lansing, while creating a strong culture that is client and employee based, which has resulted in extremely low staff turnover. Peckham's business model is heavily based on contracts with the Federal Government through the AbilityOne program. Read more about Peckham at their web site: www.peckham.org

Scaling Choice: Organic growth almost exclusively in Lansing for many years, but recent decisions have been made to accept contract work in other states.

Growth over the past decade: In fiscal year 2002, Peckham's revenues were $46.1 million. By fiscal year 2011, revenues had grown to $192.3 million.

Recap

In this introductory chapter, you've started your journey toward being a nonprofit full of smart stewards. I've described the nonprofit nirvana I hope you can move toward, and given you some initial things to think about as you proceed through the book.

I told you that the book is for nonprofit decision makers, and emphasized that there are more of them in your organization than you may think. We looked at why I think this book is needed now, and how many nonprofits are moving forward, growing, and expanding while others are biding their time. In both cases, good decisions are needed at the board, senior staff, and line of service levels.

I then gave you a long list of benefits that will accrue to you if you read the entire book, and suggested some ways to get more out of the book, particularly by reading the book in teams and using the discussion questions that follow each chapter.

Next, we went through a brief thumbnail review of each chapter in the book, giving you the briefest preview of what's to come.

Finally, I introduced you to our three case nonprofits, GING, Lakeview, and Peckham. You'll be visiting with them often in the coming chapters.

I hope that you're eager to turn the page and get started. And where we'll start is at the beginning, with the Keys to Smart Stewardship. Enjoy your reading.

CHAPTER 2

The Keys to Smart Stewardship for Your Nonprofit

Chapter Thumbnail

Overview

As we start down the path to Smart Stewardship, we have to begin with some context setting. In this chapter, we'll dive down into what may seem to some readers to be basic ideas about your nonprofit and your role in it. I beg to differ; they're not basic, they're profound. Why? Because if you adopt them and embrace them as part of both your strategic and day-to-day decision making, they will not only improve the way your nonprofit provides mission, they will change the way that you, your staff, and board see your organization's role in your community.

In the remainder of the book (after this chapter) I'll be giving you a lot of how-tos. We'll go over ideas on innovation, core competence, growth, scaling, and the like. Those ideas, of and by themselves, will be *interesting*. But when you put them in the context of the philosophies you'll find in this chapter, they will be *meaningful*. There's a larger lesson here as well: The more context you can give people when you inform them of events, or delegate work, or ask for input on a problem, the better. More on that later.

13

In this chapter, we'll start where we always should, with your mission. I'll show you why your mission is your most valuable asset, four key mission-related questions that should guide you on a day-to-day basis, and how to incorporate mission more into your deliberations and meetings. Then, we'll turn to my definition of stewardship, and why Smart Stewards are the most effective managers of a nonprofit's resources.

Next we'll talk about money, both as an enabler of mission, and why regular and consistent profit is the only way to do more mission. And you want to do more mission, right?

After that, we'll look at why constant innovation is so crucial to Smart Stewardship, and how innovation and change need to be both led *and* followed. Then, we'll turn to an important foundation for Smart Stewardship, your common decision framework. As you'll see, developing and consistently using this framework is a huge initial step toward being Smart Stewards.

Finally, we'll touch on the last key to Smart Stewardship, engaging everyone. The more people we ask, the more people we tell, the more people we engage in our mission, the stronger we become. This means sharing more information more freely than you may have in the past. This also means asking (really asking, not some token survey) people for their input, people you might never have asked in the past.

By the end of the chapter, you'll have been exposed to the keys to Smart Stewardship and be ready to move through the chapters that follow with the context you need to put what you'll learn into more effective action.

It Always Starts with Your Mission

Let's start with the end point, the bottom line, the ultimate outcome. Why? Because the starting point and the end point for any nonprofit should always be the same: the mission. In your day-to-day discussions, your week-to-week decisions, your five-year strategy, the result of all your deliberations should always come down to one or more of the following outcomes:

- more mission
- better mission
- more effective mission
- more efficient mission

Sounds pretty straightforward, right? Wouldn't we all like to be able to do this every day, every decision, every meeting with our board and staff?

While we might like to in theory, in the real world, it's *not* easy, as any seasoned nonprofit manager will tell you. There are widely varying opinions about most decisions in nearly all organizations. The board may want to go one way, while the staff may want to take a different path. Within the employees, line staff may see a different set of priorities than the management team, due to their very different perspectives. Volunteers, funders, donors, and, of course, the people you serve all have their ideas, and each comes from a different place, even in situations where everyone agrees on the organization's mission and values (not always the case, trust me). All of these reasons are why we're going to examine common decision-making strategies starting in the next chapter.

For now, though, let's look at each of those four seemingly simple outcomes in a bit more depth.

More Mission

A decision that results in your organization doing more mission can result in that mission increase in the short term, or down the road. For example, a counseling service might decide to add longer hours, a school might add a classroom and associated staff, and a low-income housing developer could choose to add 12 new units. These kinds of choices are pretty straightforward. But just longer-term strategy that results in more mission could be a capital fund drive that will allow your organization to be able to afford the space to do more mission, or a new web site upgrade that will allow people to more easily sign up for services (or even get some of their services online).

 HANDS-ON: When you rationalize a decision based on planned increases in mission output, always try to quantify how much more mission you expect to see, and when you expect to see it. Thus, the counseling service that adds longer hours might expect a 5 percent increase in services starting in the next 60 days, while the capital fund drive might result in doubling mission output, but not for three or four years down the road. In either case, as you, your staff, and board look at the return on investment you should be getting, having a specific expected outcome is key. We'll talk much more about return on investment in a few pages. ■

Better Mission

Doing more missions is wonderful, but just as important is doing the mission you're already churning out at a higher level of quality. That's better mission. We'll discuss core competencies (what your nonprofit is really good at) in Chapter 5, but for now, let's examine some decisions that could improve quality. Of course, developing and using a quality assurance policy is one such decision, but so is investing more in staff education and life-long learning, engaging in site visits at other peer organizations, joining and being active in a professional association, or deciding to participate in an accreditation process in your organization's field.

Most importantly, just saying in your values statement "Our nonprofit will be a world-class organization" does not by itself make it so. You have to decide to invest the time, the talent, and the treasure to do so.

More Effective Mission

The final two outcomes, "More Effective Mission" and "More Efficient Mission," sound similar but they are not (and are often confused), and I want to deal with what I will suggest is the more important of the two first.

A more effective mission outcome is one that has more lasting effect in whatever way your nonprofit views the optimal outcome. It is described very well in the old adage "Feed a person a fish, and they eat for a day. Teach the person to fish and they eat for a lifetime." Thus the nonprofit that feeds 1 or 100 people a fish has a higher volume but not a very effective outcome. The same nonprofit deciding to invest in fishing classes may well have found a more effective use of their resources.

 FOR EXAMPLE: In *Begging for Change*, Robert Eggar's wonderful book on the nonprofit sector, Eggar notes that at DC Kitchens, the nonprofit he founded to deal with hunger in the District of Columbia, "I realized that I could feed 10 people or 1000 people, but if I fed the same person year after year, I had failed."

Eggar came to this realization only after his food kitchen was serving thousands of meals. He had to reflect on how to do the most good, how to be most effective in his mission provision. His solution was to use his facilities to teach homeless and unemployed people to cook, and in the teaching, prepare food for other soup kitchens. The model has won all kinds of awards, but more importantly, given people life skills that they otherwise would not have had. ■

The moral here is that becoming more effective is usually not something that we figure out at the beginning of providing a service; it's a mid-stream epiphany. It requires that we not get complacent about how much good we're doing but are constantly looking for new ways to improve our outcome. It mandates that we look at what our peer organizations are doing and look outside our field to apply lessons learned in other areas of service. It requires constant and true innovation, which will be our topic in Chapter 7.

More Efficient Mission

Efficiency is good, as long as it doesn't affect quality and effectiveness. And, as a steward, since our job is to get the most high-quality mission out the door every day with all the resources we have, we should be as efficient as we possibly can be. This requires that we are also innovative and reflective, looking at best practices and trying to wring as much mission out of every dime that we can.

Some efficiencies come from technology (largely financial management, human resources (HR), and communications benefits for most nonprofits) but tech is not the end-all solution to making services more efficient for most nonprofits.

FOR EXAMPLE: There is no question that automated answering systems are efficient for the companies that use them. If you call and talk to or interact with a machine it is much, much less expensive than having you talk to a real person. Similarly, if that person is in India or somewhere else where labor costs are cheap, it's even less expensive for the company.

But is it effective as well? You see, efficiency can only be beneficial if it is *also* effective (in this case in answering your questions). But what automated answering machines (as well as offshore customer call centers) have wrought is legions of furious, frustrated customers who tell all their friends and co-workers how angry they are at the company that they first called for help. ■

So, beware implementing efficiencies without thinking through how they will affect the people you need to move your mission forward: your staff, board, funders, donors, and, of course, the people you serve.

HANDS ON: With any significant change or "improvement" always run the idea and its impacts by the people who will be effected before you decide to move ahead. In Chapter 7 on Innovation, I'll term this "putting more neurons on the problem." In cases of hoped-for efficiencies, asking people from throughout the organization for input will give you a variety of different perspectives, which may save you from having your "improvement" be a disaster. ■

Sometimes, ideas of how to measure our efficiency get us into trouble as well. We tend to measure what's easy, which can result in our measuring and valuing activity rather than quality. A counselor who is evaluated on seeing at least 20 people a shift (up from an average of 17 last month) may well begin to value volume over quality, or just as likely resent the management team as people "who don't care about services . . . they just want us to treat our clients like numbers so we can get reimbursed." So, be careful, and ask widely before moving ahead.

Speaking of measuring the wrong thing, there's one more example of an intended efficiency measure that has wrought huge damage on the non-profit sector that I want to recount as a cautionary tale.

 FOR EXAMPLE: The late 1990s brought the advent of a number of online watchdog web sites such as Guidestar and Charity Navigator. Their mission: To provide donors and funders easy comparative access to data about which nonprofits were being most efficient and effective. On the surface, this was (and, frankly, still is) a great idea. More transparency in the sector is a great thing. The problem was how to measure efficiency across the board. What's the metric that makes sense? The same issue confronted these groups about effectiveness, which is much, much harder to measure, so they understandably started with efficiency.

And, understandably as well, the groups asked funders what they'd like to see measured. The problem was, funders also wanted to fund the most efficient grantees, but had unfortunately begun to settle on a metric called "administrative percentage." Admin percent, or admin load, as it was often called, was most easily measured by looking at expenses that were not direct-service provision costs. Thus, for many organizations, all the management team salaries and benefits, all HR for them, all information technology (IT), all continuing education, travel, rent, insurance, and so on fell into this category. As more and more funders (and the online groups) began measuring admin costs, a set of standard acceptable percentages popped up. Some funders began telling grantees that an admin load over 10 or 12 percent was unacceptable. For some the magic number became 14 percent. This was not just the new priority for foundations or corporations (although most jumped in) but also considered a best practice in funding by state and local governments.

The results have been disastrous. Most nonprofits began to be extremely hesitant about adding any new administrator, or about improving their web site, or funding staff education. The relentless drive to make the "good" admin percentage has resulted in most nonprofits in the United States under administered, harming growth, affecting quality, and in general, making the nonprofit sector weaker, not more efficient.

And here's the worst part. Measuring admin load is a *totally valueless metric*, particularly if you are deciding to fund Nonprofit A over Nonprofit B. It tells the funder nothing of value. Think of going to a car dealership and deciding to buy one car over another based on its weight. How much one car weighs over another is a comparative and measurable number, sure. But does it have any value to you as an owner? Fuel efficiency (related to weight, but not the same) has some value, but weight? Not so much.

The same is true with admin load. It's easy to measure and sounds good, but any funder who pushes it as a meaningful measure has never run an organization (or taken a business finance course). Worse, the percentages picked (I suspect essentially out of the air) by the funders are cripplingly low and unrealistic.

It's the best (or worst, depending on your perspective) example I have of measuring the wrong thing in the quest for more efficiency. ■

Let's end our discussion of efficiency to say this: Being efficient in mission-provision is a good thing, as long as it doesn't negatively affect quality or effectiveness. Think efficiency measures through carefully, ask widely before implementing and monitor outcomes to make sure that the Law of Unintended Consequences hasn't snuck up on you.

To reiterate, all your decisions should result in one (or better, more than one) of the outcomes listed above. And, since everyone in your organization, board, staff, and non-governing volunteers wants to do the best mission possible, getting your decisions to accomplish one or more of the four mission outcomes *should* be pretty easy.

But it's NOT easy, as any seasoned nonprofit manager will tell you. As I noted in the introduction to this chapter, there are widely varying opinions in most organizations about the best ways to proceed, what's most efficient or most effective. In organizations that enable and encourage healthy debate, board, staff, non-governing volunteers, funders, donors, and, of course, the people you serve all have their ideas—and make their opinions known, even in situations where everyone agrees on the organization's mission and values (not always the case, trust me).

These differences, when they appear, can be distracting and divisive. Hear me clearly, frank discussions, what a friend of mine marvelously calls "vigorous fellowship," are vital to any healthy organizations. You want forums where people speak their mind, offer their insights, and defend their positions. But if you agree on some key tenets, what we're labeling the keys to smart stewardship, you'll focus your discussions in a way that ends with your nonprofit being more mission-capable.

So let's get the keys on the table. As you read these, think about each in turn carefully. If you polled your board and key staff about them would everyone agree, or would you see some discord? How close is your organization now to adopting these ideas, these keys to Smart Stewardship?

Your Mission Is, Far and Away, Your Most Valuable Asset

Your mission is worth more than your buildings, more than your bank account and, yes, worth more than your volunteers, board, or staff. Why? Because the *mission is why those people show up*. You need to use your mission as a decision tool, a marketing edge, a motivation resource, a fund-raising hook. And, while doing that you also need to protect the mission, since it's your brand. The first Key to Smart Stewardship is that everything starts and ends with the mission.

You're a Smart Steward of Other People's Stuff

I've already noted that you are a steward of your nonprofit, whether you're a staff member, chief executive officer (CEO), volunteer, or governing volunteer. Your job is to get the most mission out the door every day with the resources in hand. Nice thought. But let's examine the term *steward*. A steward is someone who manages *someone else's* resources. In this case, you are responsible for the resources of the nonprofit, and since no one but the community "owns" the nonprofit, you're really in charge of the resources that the community has entrusted the organization with.

In other words, it's not your stuff.

It's not *your* nonprofit, it's the community's. It's not *your* endowment, it's funds the community has trusted you to pursue mission with. *Your* building? Technically owned by your 501(c)(3), but since the nonprofit is really the community's . . . you get the idea.

Oddly enough, this puts even more pressure and responsibility on your shoulders. Why? Because it's not your stuff.

 FOR EXAMPLE: All of us have our way of driving an automobile. Some of us pay close attention to every stop sign, some of us, uh, roll through one now and again. Some are vigilant about the speed limit, some use those numbers as rough guidelines. But I think it's safe to say that when we borrow a friend's car, we are much, much safer drivers. Why? Because the car we're in is not ours. ■

So our second key is that our stewardship is of other people's stuff.

Money Matters

Boy, does it ever. I've said this probably 10,000 times to audiences and classes: "The First rule of nonprofits is "Mission, Mission, and More Mission," but the Second rule is "No Money, No Mission." Mission is always first, but money is a very, very close second.

There is *no* room (none) in a Smart Stewardship organization for a philosophy that says "We have such a wonderful mission, we should focus on that and not really worry too much about money and accounting and all that stuff." Why? Because *money matters*. How you acquire the money, allocate the money, spend the money, control the money, and account for the money—it all matters. And doing all those things is part of a steward's job. It may not be as much fun as providing mission, but it's just as integral to your stewardship role.

Let's drill down a bit more. If you have people who still think of mission as holy and money as tainted, ask them this: "Do you want to do high quality mission next year?" Of course they do. So, remind them of this truth: "**Money is the enabler of mission**." Money is needed to do mission, even in totally volunteer-run organizations. That said, money is *only* the enabler of mission, not the priority in and of itself. Mission first, but. . . .

Now, ask that same person or group this: "Would you like to do *more* high quality mission next year?" And most, if not all of them will say yes, of course we do. If so, tell them this next truth: "**Profit is the enabler of more mission**." If you want your organization to grow, you must make money. Why? Because growth requires what the business community calls "working capital" and without it, you run out of cash really, really fast. So if you want to expand your mission, you have to embrace profits on your Income and Expense statements. And that last bit is what drives some board members, some funders, and some staff slightly nuts.

We'll talk a lot more about this when we discuss growth. For now, remember that you can't grow if you don't make money. Which leads nicely into our next key.

Your Nonprofit Is Not a Charity. Your Nonprofit Is a Mission-based Business.

Your organization is in the business of doing mission. Mission first. But a mission-based business acts in a businesslike manner. It uses all the tools at its disposal, including business skills like marketing, accounting, human resources, strategic planning, feasibility studies, and so on to do more mission.

A steward of a mission-based business looks at all the expenditures of the organization as **investments in mission**. If you are investing in option

A (say, expanding to the next county) versus option B (expanding in your current locale) you should evaluate your return on that investment. That's what all businesses do.

Except in the nonprofit world, we have *two* returns to evaluate. The first return, just as in a for-profit business, is the **financial return**. How much is this going to cost? Will it make money or lose money? How much? If it's making money, how soon (if ever) will we recover our investment? This part is pretty straightforward.

The second return is tougher to measure: **mission return**. How much mission will option A do versus option B and how soon? In the example I chose (expansion here versus expansion there), this is pretty easy to measure. But some comparisons are very tough. For a private school, is it better to add more field trips, or add an additional classroom? For a place of worship, is it better to add an evening worship service or send 30 people on a mission trip overseas? For a museum, should they open more hours, or pay for a new traveling exhibit? None of these are apples-to-apples comparisons, and thus are difficult to assess, which is why, when we talk about the decision tree in Chapter 3, we'll see how such assessments are done in the light of mission, values, priorities, the strategic plan, and so on.

Even though it's difficult, you do need to look at *both* the financial and mission return on your investment. Why? Because even though we've seen that profit is the enabler of more mission, profit is not needed, reasonable, likely, or even possible for some services your nonprofit will and should provide. There are things in your community that need doing, people that need help, services that are lacking, and sometimes those services simply can't be provided at a profit . . . and you should still do them *if the mission return is high.*

Thus, a low financial return can be balanced by a high mission return. On the other hand, if there is a low mission return for a project, it should certainly make money.

 FOR EXAMPLE: Think of a soup kitchen, one where hungry people come to eat. I know your mission rocks, but I challenge you to tell me that what you do is MORE mission-rich than feeding the hungry. Equally mission-rich, maybe, but I doubt you can claim *higher* mission ground. So, a nonprofit that runs the soup kitchen is doing something very mission-rich, but very money poor—it can't charge people for the food—that would be contrary to the entire idea of the organization. Should it continue? Of course. Mission rich, money poor is fine, IF it's a priority of the strategic plan, IF there are other services that make money, and so on. ■

FOR EXAMPLE: Now, can you think of an outreach service that most nonprofits invest (sometimes significant) assets in that does no mission? Think through your organization first, then expand that process to five other nonprofits. I'll almost guarantee that at least three of them invest significant time, talent, and/or treasure in this activity. And it does no mission.

Give up? This mystery outreach is called development or fundraising. Development, of and by itself, does no mission. In fact, it *only* results in mission when the development department makes money, posts a profit, contributes to the bottom line. Since development does no mission, it must make money. Every year. ■

Let's look at this double return graphically. Exhibit 2.1 is a standard two-by-two grid that shows mission return on the x-axis (low to high) and financial return on the y-axis, again low to high. So, if your service is in the bottom left-hand corner, you have both low mission and low financial returns, which is why you are advised to "Avoid, if at all possible."

You can also see that in the upper right hand corner, even with a high mission and high financial return, you are advised to "proceed, *if* it's a core

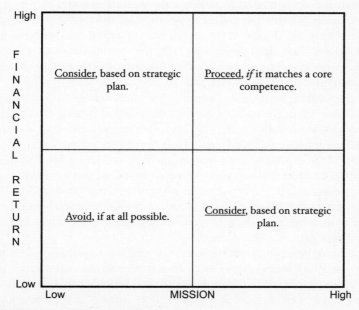

EXHIBIT 2.1 Mission Return–Financial Return

competence." We'll talk at length about doing what you do well in Chapter 5, and you'll see why it is so important to be competent from day one.

Finally Exhibit 2.1 shows us that in mixed-return situations (low mission/high financial or the opposite) you're advised to proceed IF the idea has already been carefully considered in your organization's strategic or business plan.

The double return concept will show up repeatedly in the following chapters. If you agree that your nonprofit is a mission-based business, evaluating the return on every investment is one outcome of that belief.

Again, your nonprofit is a *mission-based business*. That's our third key to Smart Stewardship.

Innovation Must Be Baked Into Your Culture

Smart Stewardship organizations are always trying to improve their array of service. It's clear that if you seek to do any of the last three mission outcomes (better mission, more effective mission, more efficient mission) you have to be innovating, in large and small ways.

It is also obvious to many managers (although not all) that they (the managers) don't have all the answers to every problem that arises. Each of us only gets 24 hours in every day. Each of us can only see any given problem from *our* perspective, *our* experience, *our* training. That is, by definition, limiting. We need to ask more people (see the following section) and make sure that innovation, trying new things, taking reasonable risks is a cultural touchstone. Innovation needs to be baked into our values, our recruiting, our evaluations, our rewards system, our conversations, and our board, staff, and committee meetings.

All innovations are risky, some more than others. And, remember, the risks we take are in an effort to be good stewards of community resources. It's not our stuff. Therefore it's important that we overlay our willingness to take risk with good feasibility studies and business-planning skills. Further, the innovation risks we take should ultimately be pointed toward an outcome of more mission, better mission, more effective mission, or more efficient mission. In my book, *Social Entrepreneurship* (John Wiley & Sons, 2000), I defined a social entrepreneur as someone who is willing "to take reasonable risk on behalf of the people the organization serves."

One more key thing about innovation, which is the subject of Chapter 7: It's not just about leadership. Certainly, a leader who is inquisitive, always learning, always considering new ways to do mission is essential. But if innovation is to be organization-wide, if everyone is to be engaged, if innovation is truly baked into the culture, then all the leaders must also be willing to listen and to follow someone else's good idea. Not all solutions must come from the management team. In fact, if they do, the organization is held back and mission potential is not reached.

Remember this mantra about innovation (apologies to John Maxwell). You, your staff, and board need to live by it: "Every idea is a good idea until we come up with the best idea. . . . and the best idea does not have to be my idea." Much, much more on this in Chapter 7, but it leads us nicely into our next key to Smart Stewardship.

You Have to Engage Everyone

I touched on this in Chapter 1, but let's review: All the easy problems in society are pretty much solved. The hard ones are left, and for the most part, they are left to nonprofits. Poverty? Let's contract that out to charitable groups. Social Justice? There must be a nonprofit that can take care of that. Addiction? Animal cruelty? Family counseling? Wounded warriors? Ditto.

These and hundreds of other of the most challenging problems in society are in our hands. And to think that just our staff, or just our board, or just our management team can solve them (or just our profession, but we'll get to that) is hubris, and hubris that is paid for by the people we serve, because we don't know it all, and we can't, by ourselves (at the board, staff, management-team level), solve the problems as well as we can if we reach out and ask.

This is easy and dangerous. Simple and messy. The more you ask, the more expectations are on you. The more you ask, the more "crazy" ideas get dumped on you and the risk of people being mad that you didn't use "their" idea increases. The more you ask, the more you open yourself (and your organization) up to criticism.

All true. But the benefits, at least in my experience with hundreds of nonprofits, outweigh the risks tenfold. Why? Because when you ask more widely, you get new ideas from different perspectives. You get solutions you couldn't see because of your training, experience, and viewpoint. Thus, the question becomes this: In your deliberations and problems solving are you asking enough people? For service delivery problems, are you asking your line staff (even the newest hires) and the people you serve? For improvements in internal policies, are you including representatives from all levels of the organization? We all know the overused term "think outside the box," but are you reading and meeting outside the box as well?

HANDS ON: I'm always intrigued with stories of how a biologist solved a 10-year-long puzzle by insights gained when she had coffee with an astronomer, explained her conundrum, and the astronomer said, "Well, we have a sort of similar problem . . . why don't you try this? . . . " In a wonderful article in *Wired* a few years back on "What to Do When Things Go Wrong" the authors, in their checklist, included this suggestion: "**Ask the Ignorant**". Not ignorant in IQ, but ignorant in your profession.

I love that, and realized when I read it that I do it all the time, with my kids, with my wife, with my friends in other fields. Simply by having to explain your issue to someone outside the field, you are forced to break it down into simple parts. You have to get away from jargon and can't make assumptions. Sometimes this results in your seeing the solution yourself, but more often, by asking someone outside your field, and then really listening, you can find that nugget, that insight that you are blind to because you are so close.

Go ahead, ask the "ignorant"—just don't call them that! ∎

In Chapter 7 on Innovation, we'll recount many stories about just this phenomenon, but for now, go with me on this; unless you are very, very unusual as an organization, you need to ask more people to the decision-making and innovation party. When you do, you'll have more ideas, and those ideas will need some organization. Which leads perfectly into our seventh and culminating key to Smart Stewardship.

You Need a Common Strategy and Decision Process

If you are surprised that this is one of the keys to Smart Stewardship, you haven't been paying attention up to this point. The need for a common strategy and decision process that your board, management team, and staff can use should be clearly evident by now.

Let's review quickly why this is key. First, with all your new innovative ideas coming from all the people you are involving, you need to stay focused on your four mission outcomes. A decision process can help discipline you to do that. Next, you're taking risks and need to evaluate both financial and mission returns. Money matters but mission matters more, so what's the return in each area? Again, a decision process can help make sure that neither return overwhelms the other; that they stay in balance. Remember, too much mission, not enough money, you're out of business and not doing anyone any good. Too much money, not enough mission, well, you're just a business, not a mission-based business. No fun in that.

Third, with all the new input you are getting and all the innovative ideas that are being generated you want everyone to be looking at the same set of criteria on how to move forward and bring ideas up the food chain when necessary.

 HANDS ON: A common decision format is terrific for delegation and pushing decisions as far down in the organization as possible. If senior managers, line managers, the CEO, and the board are all using a common framework, less people come to you with ideas or solutions that violate your core principles. Once you develop your decision tree, let everyone see it, and urge/cajole/require everyone to use it. You'll have less conflict and more consensus around how to move forward. ■

The next chapter (Chapter 3) is entirely dedicated to the subject of the decision tree, but I want to leave you with one important thought: A decision framework should balance keeping the organization true to its mission and values, taking reasonable risks, and evaluating both mission and financial return, but it should not constrict the idea generation from all parties that is so important to organizational excellence. You don't want your framework to be a box no one is allowed to think outside. And the tendency is to do just that. I'll show you how to avoid that trap in Chapter 3.

Now you've seen the seven keys to Smart Stewardship. I hope you like them and agree with them. If you do, you're going to have a much easier time reading and engaging with the rest of the book. I also hope that as your read through this chapter that none of these keys produced a response like: "Ahhhh, *that* one's going to be a problem with my board (staff/community)." But, if it did, the following chapters will give you the tools to overcome such resistance. If you didn't have any negative reactions, that's great. You'll be able to move ahead more quickly, but remember, don't assume everyone is on board. Have some discussions about my keys with your board and staff soon.

The bottom line is that when your entire staff, board, and volunteer cadre become Smart Stewards, your mission, and the people it serves, benefit.

Recap

In this chapter, you learned about the seven Keys to Smart Stewardship. To recount, these are:

1. Your Mission is Far and Away, Your Most Valuable Asset
2. You're a Smart Steward of Other People's Stuff

3. Money Matters
4. Your Nonprofit Is Not a Charity, It's a Mission-Based Business
5. Innovation Must Be Baked Into Your Culture
6. You Have to Engage Everyone
7. You Need a Common Strategy and Decision Process

You learned why these keys are true, how they are related, and, in most cases, got to see some key elements of what you'll learn later in the book. All of these keys are important, but the first four are the true philosophical underpinnings of successful nonprofits. I hope you'll take the time to discuss them with your staff before moving on. Use the Discussion questions that follow to see what your staff and board (hopefully) think about them and whether they are right for your organization. Have those discussions now, if at all possible.

Once you do that, you're ready to move on to Chapter 3, where we'll take our first look at developing a decision tree, and I'll provide you with my example of just such a framework.

Discussion Questions

1. Does our organization always put mission first? How, specifically do we do that?
2. Is it as simple as more mission, better mission, more effective mission, more efficient mission? Why or why not?
3. Do we really see ourselves as a mission-based business? Or do we act more like a charity? Is that okay?
4. How do we feel about making a profit? How does our board feel? Is there a wide understanding inside the organization that "profit enables more mission"? If not, how do we help people to understand the truth in that statement?
5. Do we keep too much decision authority at the management-team level? Are we pushing innovation and decision authority deep enough in the organization? What more can we do to enable this?
6. Do we believe Peter's mantra about every idea being a good idea? Do we act that way or are we dismissive of new staff, young staff, and/or inexperienced staff's ideas?
7. Are we asking enough people their opinions and ideas? Are we taking enough time to engage widely?

CHAPTER 3

The Smart Stewardship Decision Tree

Chapter Thumbnail

Overview
Why Use a Decision Tree?
The Smart Stewardship Decision Tree
Developing Your Own Decision Tree
Recap

Overview

In Chapter 2, you learned the keys to Smart Stewardship, which gave you the foundation from which to proceed when deciding to grow your mission, keep it the same size, or align with other service providers. In this chapter, we'll talk about common decision-making formats and give you some hands-on tools to consider using. By the end of the chapter, you'll have seen the core of how to actually implement Smart Stewardship.

First, we'll talk through why to use a decision tree at all. I am strongly convinced that a common decision format helps nonprofits make better, more mission-rich decisions, make them faster, and allows better delegation of decision authority. That said, there's a risk of developing groupthink, something you do *not* want to drift into. I'll show you how to avoid that trap.

Next, I'll show you my Smart Stewardship decision tree, and we'll discuss how you might use it in your organization. This decision framework is one you'll see throughout the remainder of the book. We'll walk through it step by step, and give you a thorough overview.

Once you're oriented, we'll look at some ways to use the decision tree inside your nonprofit. I'll show you a number of examples of how organizations have used the decision tree to make better and more mission-based decisions, from the board to the line staff.

No model like this one is perfect, and no model can be applied to every nonprofit in every situation. Thus, in the last section of the chapter, I'll show you how to customize the questions and priorities in the framework for your own organization. It is something that you can do now, or better yet, as you build up experience using a decision model for your organization.

By the end of the chapter, you'll be fully versed in why a decision tree is good to use, have seen an example of a decision tree to consider, have examined a case study of a nonprofit using a decision tree, and know how to take my work and improve and customize it for your organization.

That's a lot to cover, so let's get at it.

Why Use a Decision Tree?

There are many levels of decision-making in any organization, nonprofits included. You decide things at a board level, such as strategic direction, annual budgets, target markets, and how much to invest in staff education, just to name a few. Senior management has to implement the strategies (and budgets) adopted by the board, and thus has to make lots of decisions about sequencing (what comes first, second, and third with staff so overworked), resource allocation, and mid-course corrections when things don't go exactly as planned. At the mid-management and line of service level, implementation strategies meet reality, and that interaction (some would say collision) often requires quick adaptations.

If your nonprofit has more than, say, 10 employees or volunteers, many of these decisions, particularly those at the line of service, are not made in a group or, at least, not made in a group where the chief executive officer (CEO) or board president is present. Thus you have to trust your staff and volunteers to make the right choices when they are on their own, to make decisions that result in one or more of the four outcomes we discussed in the last chapter: more mission, better mission, more efficient mission, more effective mission.

So how can a decision tree help you make better decisions? Oddly, in some cases, it will help you be able to not make the decision at all. More on that in a minute, but now let's look at the reasons to consider using a decision tree:

More consistent, mission-based decisions across the organization.
If there is one outcome that trumps all the others, this is it. By developing and using a decision matrix, you can cut the time needed to get staff (particularly new staff) up to speed as to the way

decisions are made and the key issues that need to be covered in those decisions. If the people that report to you know you'll bounce back an issue brought to you if it hasn't gone through the decision matrix first, you're likely to get better, vetted ideas brought to your door.

FOR EXAMPLE: When our kids were in school, my wife and I had an iron-clad rule about the kids bringing us papers to proof read: They couldn't bring them to us until they had read them to themselves . . . *aloud.* Why? Try it sometime. Your ears read differently than your eyes, and catch different mistakes that your eyes will gloss over. The moral here is that using a different method of checking will help make for better product. In my kids' case, it was reading their work aloud. In your staff's case it's using the decision tree to bring you a better, more fully vetted idea or recommendation. ■

In addition to inter-staff decisions, your board will know that when you bring ideas to them for policy action that you've already gone through the mission/values/capacity vetting and thus the board's discussions can focus on the policy, not the management or administrative details that sometimes distract a board (and vex a staff).

The decision tree is a backup checklist for big or very fast decisions.

If you've had to make very big decisions in your career, you've almost certainly had doubts about whether you've considered everything. "What am I forgetting?" is a concern that has kept many a non-profit manager up at night. Of course, that kind of concern is only exacerbated if the decision needs to be fast, right now, with no real time to think through the options at the pace you're most comfortable.

While you might use your decision matrix to work through day-to-day issues, it's these kinds of big choices, or the fast ones, where the decision tree can help simply by being a mental checklist (with the caution of just being a quick checklist discussed below) that helps you be sure you've touched on all the key impacts and issues.

HANDS ON: Once you develop your own decision tree, make sure you incorporate the key elements into your disaster policies. If you don't have disaster policies, now would be a great time to develop them. Disaster policies are just that: guidance for what to do in or after natural or man-made disaster situations. Often they require quick action, and thus the checklist nature of the policies (first, call these people; second, do this; third, secure this; . . .). Make sure that any elements of your decision tree that are appropriate show up in these checklists. ■

The decision tree can help with delegation and reporting.

How can you be confident that your staff will make the right decision? Particularly if your nonprofit is financially fragile, won't any decision that's wrong potentially have lasting impact? What if the people you're responsible for mess up? What happens to you, and to your mission?

Sound familiar? These are very, very common reasons/excuses as to why not to trust your staff to make decisions in your absence. Of course, you need to do just that: Trust your staff to make good decisions, because you can't be everywhere all the time. A decision tree can help in this area, simply because once it's widely in use, it gives a framework and a buffer from making really damaging decisions. It will keep *most* staff *most* days within a reasonable mission/values safety net.

And, for those managers who are leery of delegating both responsibility and authority, training their staff in the use of the decision tree, as well as the expectation of its use, can help wean such managers from looking over the shoulders of their direct reports 24/7/365.

It's important to point out that decision matrices or trees are at their best when they have been developed by a group process that is very inclusive and when staff and board are trained how to use them, and use them regularly. Some people will consider the whole idea restrictive and anti-creative, but if you cast as wide a net as possible in the matrix's development, if it is synced with your mission and values, and if you train and lead in its use, you'll be fine.

There are two dangers in using a decision tree to consider before we move on. First, there is the possibility that using a common tool like this could take you where you don't want to go: groupthink. You'll remember that one of the keys to Smart Stewardship is "Innovation Must Be Baked Into Your Culture." You don't want your decision tree to stifle innovation. Thus the questions in the decision tree must generate discussion, cause reflection, but not just become a management lockstep that squelches every new idea before it can fully gestate.

 FOR EXAMPLE: All of your organizations have (I hope) various policies that dictate behavior, push your values, provide checks and balances, and demonstrate processes that are acceptable or mandated. Financial, human resources (HR), disaster, and quality-assurance (QA) policies are examples of such policies.

Some of these policies have to be very stringent (usually financial and HR are examples of tightly worded process policies) and some are more a to-do list, such as disaster policy, which is often more a checklist of what to make sure you cover in or after a crisis.

In 1982, Tom Peters and Robert Waterman published their seminal management guide titled *In Search of Excellence*, in which they observed that the most successful organizations were what they termed "loose-tight" organizations. What this meant was that there were stringently drawn policies within which there was room to move around, be creative, try new things. Organizations that dictated behavior too tightly ("put your right foot here, your left foot there . . . ") stifled creativity and depressed employee morale. Perhaps counterintuitively, organizations that had no policies, no guidelines, that were loose-loose also had low staff morale and creativity. Why? Because there was a kind of anarchy that very few people can thrive in. ■

You want your decision tree to be loose-tight. You want to guide people to stay within the walls of your mission and values, to make sure what you're doing you are good at, to consider money and mission, but within that set of walls to be as innovative and creative as possible. It's an . . . interesting balance to strike.

The final danger to consider is that of a decision tree just becoming a mindless checklist. You have a decision to make, you look at the matrix and say, "Mission, check, values, check, money . . . well pretty much a check. Quality . . . check, I guess, capacity . . . check . . . " and simply move on without contemplating the real concerns that any checklist is supposed to help you avoid. That's why when you see the Smart Stewardship decision tree, you'll see that each area of concern (Mission, Capacity, etc.) has very detailed questions included to help/force you to discuss them thoroughly.

These are the key benefits that can accrue from developing and using a decision tree in your Smart Stewardship nonprofit. Obviously, the best way to help you see this more deeply is to look at an actual decision tree and then see how it's applied. That's next.

The Smart Stewardship Decision Tree

Exhibit 3.1 shows the Smart Stewardship decision tree for the first time. This decision tree is designed to be used for big issues and small, in relatively stable times and in crises. You can use it as a discussion starter, a checklist, or a way to make sure that everyone in your group sees the problem, the solution, and the implications consistently.

As you read through the next few pages, keep in mind that this is my decision tree, the one I use with my clients. We'll walk through the steps in detail, but as you read, consider whether or not each core question and its sub-questions are right for your organization and if you can improve on them for your unique situation. I like this decision tree and it's worked for me and my clients, but you'll see near the end of the chapter that I don't recommend just adopting this model wholesale. Customize it for your organization. You'll get more out of it, both because of the adaptation of the tool for your nonprofit and because of the process I recommend you go through to do the customization. But first, let's take an overview look at the tree, and then break it down a bit.

The Smart Stewardship decision tree has seven of what I call core questions to consider as you move through the matrix. (I know there are eight boxes, but two are closely related to capability, and so I consider them one.) The areas that these deal with in order are:

- Mission, vision, strategy
- Capability
- Capacity
- Money
- Quality
- Analysis
- Consultation

The core questions are in priority order, and it should be no surprise to anyone that mission comes first. As you move from one core question to the next, you see that, unless you can answer the question in the affirmative, you're routed to the red box which simply states "Do *not* proceed until problems are resolved." If you can answer a core question affirmatively, you move to the next core question in priority order. And, even if you answer all the questions in the affirmative, you're still urged to "Proceed with caution."

 HANDS ON: Why proceed with caution? When you get through this management wringer shouldn't you be good to go? Here, I go back to one of the keys to Smart Stewardship: You're a steward of other people's stuff. Taking reasonable risk, innovating, trying new ways to provide service are all good, but no plan holds together perfectly once you start to implement. Check, monitor, and use your benchmarks and mid-course correction options. ■

As I said earlier, one of the dangers of any checklist is tearing through it and going check, check, check, and then moving on. I tell audiences and clients all the time that one of the greatest dangers in innovation is the CEO with the "Great Idea" that is rammed through any decision tree, feasibility study, or business plan simply because it's the CEO's idea. In our decision-making process, it's equally easy to say "Of *course* my idea is mission related!" and move on—easy, and dangerous.

So, while these core questions are valuable, in each area we need a set of what I call sub-questions to make sure you have some reason to answer any or all of the core questions in the affirmative or negative. First, though, take a look at the tree as a whole. See Exhibit 3.1.

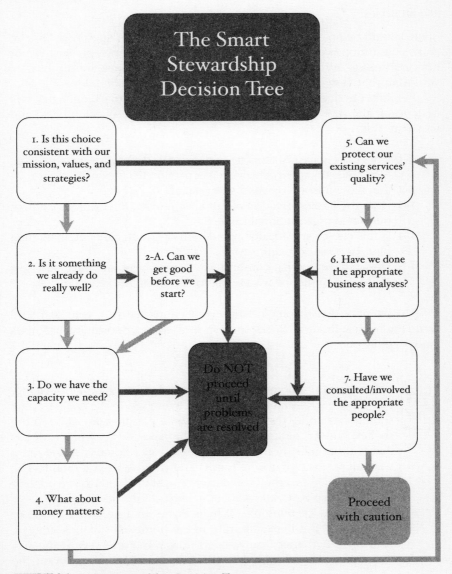

EXHIBIT 3.1 Smart Stewardship Decision Tree

As we examine each core question in a bit more depth, I'll also provide you with those sub-questions, so that you can be prepared to drill down into each area to the appropriate depth. Remember, each of the core questions will be dealt with in great detail in the remaining chapters.

Question 1: Is This Choice Consistent with Our Mission, Values, and Strategies?

There should be no doubt that this is the first of our core questions. Mission and values trump everything in a nonprofit. Remember, mission is why your nonprofit exists, it's the why of your organization; values are the how of your nonprofit, how you go about doing your great mission.

For this core question, there are four sub-questions to examine that will help you make sure you aren't falling into the "check, check, check, and move on" trap.

1-1 Does this choice result in one or more of the following: more mission, better mission, more effective mission, or more efficient mission?

1-2 Can these mission outcomes be quantified?

1-3 Does the implementation of this choice result in violation of any of our stated organizational values?

1-4 Is this choice specifically included in our strategic plan, marketing plan, or business plan?

1-5 Do we have internal consensus to move ahead and have a project champion, someone who is passionate about the idea?

The intent of the strategy question is to assure that you, your staff, and board are not just doing a "knee-jerk response" to an opportunity that arises unexpectedly.

FOR EXAMPLE: A homeless shelter in California got a call from a regular funder who said that they were interested in the shelter doing some job training for many of the same people who came to the shelter, but at a different location. The rationale the funder used is that without jobs, homeless people will stay homeless. The grant was full cost (no matching funds) and could start in a month. The staff calculated that they could use some of the funds to spread their administrative costs, and went to the board for a decision.

You may be thinking, "Why is this even a question? . . . Take the money!" But here's the rub: In the homeless shelter's strategic plan, they had specifically stated they wanted to stay at the size they were and do high-quality work. Additionally, many of the people they would have been working with at the job site are not their core market: the homeless. Finally, they didn't know anything about job counseling.

Thus this option violated the strategic plan, marketing plan, and competency (see question number two) concerns of the decision tree. The board discussed the option at great length and turned down the money. ■

HANDS ON: I have to note here that there is another twist to such a decision—a concern about making a regular funder unhappy. This is not as prevalent a problem as it is a concern. In other words, we're more paranoid than the data justify. That said, if you do turn down a funding offer, particularly from a regular funder, make sure you fully explain your decision and rationale. In the example above the funder had, in fact, paid some of the cost of the strategic plan in question. When the CEO noted that the board had opted to go with the plan rather than violate the focus that the plan described, the funder, while not thrilled, understood that the organization hadn't just turned down the funder's offer on a whim. ■

If you've already invested a lot of time and effort by developing a strategic plan which focuses your efforts on the intersection of community needs and your organization's core competencies, why violate that work whenever something drops out of the sky?

This is not to say that you can never, ever do something new or unexpected, or accommodate a new technology or trend. If that was the case, any nonprofit that developed a strategic or marketing plan in 2008 would not have been on Twitter in 2010. But the discussions, analyses, choices, and consensus building that hopefully were part of your strategic and marketing plan development should not be abandoned in a heartbeat to chase the money.

Finally, the question about consensus and a champion is crucial. If you haven't gotten internal consensus on your management team, you probably should wait a while. Assuming you hired and trust your team, there's almost always a good reason someone is holding back, even if they can't quite put their finger on it.

FOR EXAMPLE: At Peckham, both consensus and a champion are crucial. "Without an internal champion, our projects just don't move ahead," their chief operating officer (COO) told me. "We need someone to take the project and run with it, and if no one is passionate enough to do that, we drop it, at least for the time being." ■

When starting anything new, you are almost by definition going to be asking at least some of your senior and mid-level managers to do more. Get their consensus first.

Mission and values is the entire topic for Chapter 4, so you'll see a lot more then. For now, if you can answer all of the sub-questions positively, then you can move on to our second core question.

Question 2: Is It Something We Already Do Really Well?

Question 2a: If Not, Can We Get Good Before We Start? Core competence is one of the dirty little secrets of the nonprofit world. When you clear out all the smoke, nonprofits are really, really, really *good* at *some* services. They are also really, really *adequate* at many others. Much of this comes from steadily less-adequate funding, which whittles away at things like adequate administration, continuing education, even accreditation in the quest to have lower admin costs. But some of the responsibility for this falls on staff and board who either make the Faustian bargain that doing so-so work is better than none at all, or have been doing what they're doing the way they are doing it for so long they don't realize it's no longer best, or even good, practice.

I disagree with the notion that adequate services are acceptable. I think the people you serve deserve to be served well, and served well every day. That's the reason for this core question and its secondary core question. If you're thinking about doing something, are you good at it now, or if you aren't, can you get good (learn or buy the expertise) before you start? In short, is your bar high on competence and quality?

Before we get into our sub-questions, let's look at why I use the phrase " . . . already do really well." Because for areas you are entering or expanding, I want you to be core competent from day one, not day 300. In times gone by, learning some new service skill on the job was accepted and appropriate for many charities. No longer.

Let's look at our sub-questions:

2-1 Do we already hold any available accreditation in the area of service?

2-2 Do we have (and fully follow) a quality-assurance plan for this area of service?

2-3 Are we funding continuing education for staff in this area of service?

2-4 If the service we are considering is new for our organization, can we hire an expert to run the service?

2-5 If the service we are considering is not a core competency, can we expend resources to attain full competency within the next 12 months?

Obviously, if the service you are considering starting or expanding is new, sub-questions 2-1, 2-2, and 2-3 are moot, and so the last two fall into play. Alternately, if your answers to the first three sub-questions are positive, the final two sub-questions don't really matter.

Core competence will be one of the two subjects covered in Chapter 5. As with our first core question, if you can answer the sub-questions to number two in the affirmative, then you move on to core question number three.

Question 3: Do We Have the Capacity We Need?

Our third core question focuses on ideas or decisions where you are considering growing: Adding services, expanding the kinds of people you serve, the ways you serve them, the locations where you provide services, even the time of day or number of days you are open for business. Inherent to this is the issue of having enough space and resources (other than cash, which is our next core question) to handle growth.

Do you have enough information technology (IT) to handle all the new transactions? Is your HR staff adequate for new hires? Do you have enough physical space? Adequate transportation? What about management and supervision capacity?

Alternately, if you're in a financial-reduction crisis and shrinking rapidly, you need to consider ways to make sure that you retain adequate capacity to do all the things you'll still need to do after your ramp down.

Having (or gearing up) adequate capacity will not only greatly affect your likelihood of success, it will also significantly impact your ability to keep current (and new) quality high, which we'll look at in core question number five. And, while I realize that doing your business analyses (feasibility studies and business plans, which are covered in core question number six) should give you guidance on your capacity needs, I put this issue third, because it is so crucial and so often forgotten in the thrill of service expansion.

One other thing: Even if you are not considering expansion or shrinking rapidly, this core-question should force you to look at your current capacity. Remember I noted in Chapter 2 that most nonprofits are under-administered as a result of all the hammering from funders about admin costs. That's still true, and I would observe that many nonprofits are also under-teched (lacking in adequate IT), and crowded in terms of space. Thus, use this core question to reexamine the capacity you currently have, even if you're not considering rapid (or even any) growth.

We'll talk a lot more about capacity in Chapter 5, but let's quickly look at our sub-questions before we move on:

3-1 Is our physical space adequate for our programs, and do we have enough room to grow?

3-2 Is our current space physically safe for staff, volunteers, and the people we serve?

3-3 Is our IT (staff, hardware, software) capable of meeting our current and future needs (as outlined in our strategic and marketing plans)?

3-4 Do we have the HR capacity to grow?

3-5 Does our current management structure allow for the growth we anticipate or are currently considering?

By now, you know the drill: Answer these questions in the affirmative and you get to move on. If not, fix the issues that are raised before you proceed.

Question 4: What about Money Matters?

We started our discussion of cash with the Third Key to Smart Stewardship: "Money Matters." There, I told you that while *"Money Enables Mission,"* *"Profits Enable More Mission."* Thus, if you want to grow, or improve services you have to have made money in the past to fund the growth or improvement that you want to have now. Cash invested in growth is called *working capital*, which is defined as the funds you spend between the time you provide services or make a product until you get paid. The faster you grow, the more working capital you need. The longer it takes to get paid for a service, the more working capital you need.

 HANDS ON: This is why nonprofits who budget year after year to break even, yet want to grow, are always, always out of cash. Growth sucks up cash like a giant vacuum cleaner. Breaking even as a permanent budget policy is *not* Smart Stewardship. ■

Thus, if you are cash short, you shouldn't even think about growing until you've made a profit (either through payments for services or development receipts) and expect to continue to be profitable.

Also, you need to remember that any decision to spend money is an investment decision. This means that you need to measure your return on that investment, and as you'll learn in Chapter 6, when we cover the issue of money in detail, you have not only a financial return to measure but also a mission return to measure.

 HANDS ON: From this moment on, I want you to think of all the expenditures in your budget not as a bad thing (I know you prefer income to expenses!) but as *investments in mission*. Hold on to that concept, and we'll go into it more in Chapter 6. ■

What are our sub-questions for this core question? Here they are:

4-1 Do we have a cash flow projection for our entire organization that shows receipts and disbursements for six months into the future?

4-2 Have we included the cash flow projection (as opposed to budget costs, which are usually done on an accrual basis) for the issue under consideration?

4-3 Are we funding this issue/service from reserves?

4-4 If we're funding from debt, is the item we're borrowing for making an internal profit?

4-5 If we're projecting to lose money (cash or accrual) on this service/issue, have we made a mission-driven decision to do so?

NOTE: If some of the terminology in these sub-questions is foreign to you, don't worry. We'll discuss why these issues are so important in Chapter 6.

Question 5: Can We Protect Our Existing Services' Quality?

One of the repeating mantras of this book is that with any growth strategy the two things most organizations (nonprofit and for-profit) risk running out of are cash and quality. Core question number four covered the cash part, and with this core question we examine quality. We've already shown you that being more than just adequate in services is essential, but even nonprofits that are superb at what they do put quality at risk in major change scenarios. It may be a morale issue, or one of straining every resource in the organization (do you remember the concern about capacity?), or a simple and understandable staffing change.

 FOR EXAMPLE: Your organization decides to expand existing, high-quality services to a new location. As you think this through, you have to decide who to send to the new location to get it up and running. Who do you assign? Your worst staff person? A middle-of-the-road employee? No, you send your best person. And, by doing so, *you take your best person away* from your current location. What happens to quality at the current site? ■

That's the question.

Organizations that are normally focused on quality, that have sought and attained appropriate accreditation, that have QA policies, that tout quality in their values, that reward staff based on quality metrics are less likely to have a problem than those that give a passing glance at their quality once a year.

I should note here that it isn't just growth decisions that can cause quality strains. What if you send that same great staff person to an intense two-week nonprofit management program? What if you reorganize your management team, and that great staff person is now further away from the line of service and less able to regularly check on quality? And there is quality not just in service, but also in management and governance.

 FOR EXAMPLE: A center for persons with disabilities in New England, which was accredited by both the state in which they operated and a national accrediting body, was having trouble finding and keeping great board members. Over the years, they had been losing good members to age, term limits, and new jobs. At the same time, like so many nonprofits, they were having an increasingly difficult time recruiting new board members.

Their decision was to go from a straight term-limit model where any member had a maximum of two three year terms, to a modified model, where some exceptional members could stay longer. This made sense to them, and helped the problem, but violated the accreditation regulations at both the state and national level . . . something they didn't realize until their accreditation was up for renewal. ■

If your nonprofit cares about quality in all its forms, it has to be part of your regular decision checklist. And, you need some sub-questions to drill down further, so here they are.

5-1 Have we talked to line staff (or managers) about how this decision could affect their ability to do excellent services and received their feedback?
5-2 Have we checked with any accreditation regulations to make sure we're within the guidelines set for quality?
5-3 Have we reviewed our own quality assurance manual for the same thing?
5-4 Do we have current quality benchmarks that allow us to do a quality comparison in six months?

One more caution: You may remember the Ford Motor Company slogan from the late 1980s: "Quality is Job One!" Nice words but, at the time, the company didn't back them up with well-designed or competently assembled vehicles. Talking about quality is fine, but it needs to be backed up with actions from the line of service to the CEO and board of directors.

Question 6: Have We Done the Appropriate Business Analyses?

Each different decision will need a different level of analysis. For some, a simple cash-flow adjustment will do. For others, you'll need a full business plan. For some decisions, no real financial implication exists, as in the case of the board of directors' terms we looked at earlier.

That's why this core question has the word "appropriate" in it. The danger is that, in an effort to move an idea forward, the management team will pick the easiest, quickest business analysis and move on.

What are some examples of *business analyses?* Let's look at a few, give you a good definition of each, and some examples of when you might use them in the decision-making process.

Cash-Flow Projection　　Not the statement of cash flows in your organization's audit, this is a projection of receipts and disbursements on an every-two-week basis for six months into the future. It's normally updated every two weeks. How your decision affects the cash flow for the organization is the minimal analysis you should do.

Working Capital Analysis　　This is closely related to the cash-flow analysis. Remember that working capital is the cash you use between the time you produce a product or service and the time you get paid. We'll discuss an example of working capital in Chapter 6. If your decision is about growth or expanding, you absolutely need to do a working capital analysis.

Market Assessment　　Which service markets do you want to focus on? How about volunteer markets? Donor markets? Market assessment is a basic part of any marketing plan (and thus of your strategic plan). Do your target markets like you now? Do they even know your nonprofit exists? Have they asked for any change or expansion you are considering? If your decision has to do with a new market, or an expansion, you want to do this kind of analysis.

Feasibility Study　　A feasibility study is a big piece of work, but it can ward off disaster if you listen to the numbers. The key question here is this: Does your market want what you're selling/providing in the way you're providing it, in the location and at the time you're providing it, for the price you're providing it? This analysis is crucial if you're expanding an existing service to a new community or to a new demographic.

Business Plan　　The mother lode of analyses, a business plan is the longest and most involved of any of the work listed here. It's the language of business, and your board should be asking you to see a business plan for really big projects. The difference between a feasibility study and a business plan is that a feasibility study is trying to answer the question "Can we do this?", while a business plan is saying "Here's what we're going to do and why."

With those thumbnail descriptions in the back of your mind, let's look at the sub-questions for this core question:

6-1 Did I/we ask at least three people which business analysis (if any) would be best for this decision?

6-2 Once we completed any needed analysis, did we run our work by at least two other people to get consensus on our conclusion?

6-3 Did we examine both the financial and mission returns of our investment for this decision?

6-4 Is there an appropriate board committee that should look at this issue?

Don't shy away from the analyses: They'll take anything from a few minutes to a couple of weeks to complete, but they can save you a ton of grief. Another method of avoiding grief in our decisions is to get as many perspectives on the idea as possible, which leads us to our last core question.

Question 7: Have We Consulted/Involved the Appropriate People?

Our final core question is inspired by one of the Keys to Smart Stewardship that told you "You Need to Engage Everyone." In general, until you really get the idea of this particular key, until it becomes comfortable and natural for you, the basic idea is "ask more people than you have in the past."

Of course, who you should ask in any decision will vary greatly. You noted in core question six that one of the sub-questions was "Did I/we ask at least three people . . . ." and that was just to make sure you didn't skate on the level of analysis needed. More is almost always better, but you don't need to ask everyone for every decision.

Who should be asked or consulted? Depending on the issue, it could be one or more of the following:

- The board of directors (or appropriate committee of the board)
- An internal staff committee (hopefully with representation from all levels of management)
- The people you serve (not all of them, but a representative sample)
- Funders (not for permission, but for input)
- The community (other nonprofits and stakeholders)
- Consultants (only in cases where you need one-time expertise or a truly objective viewpoint)

And, as you'll note, you don't have to ask all of any group. For example, a representative sample of the people you serve, or having10 line staff out of 100 in a focus group will suffice in many cases, as will informal asking of people on an intermittent basis.

 HANDS ON: Once you start to develop a culture where "Every idea is a good idea until we find the best idea . . . " this will become much easier. If, until now, the organization has a history of keeping both information and decisions sequestered within the management team, expect some suspicion and resistance at first. Over time, and with consistent leadership in this area, more and more people will begin to engage. You'll never get everyone, but that's not the point. The point is to offer engagement in the decision process to anyone interested. As you'll find I say repeatedly in Chapter 7, *put more neurons on the problem.* ∎

Let's look at our sub-questions for this core question. They're pretty straightforward.

7-1 For a policy-level decision, did we consult the board or appropriate board committee?

7-2 For an internal decision, did we consult the manager of the program?

7-3 For an internal decision, did we consult the staff affected by the decision?

7-4 For any decision that results in a change to service, did we consult the people we serve with that service?

7-5 If appropriate, did we run this idea/change past external stakeholders?

This or any decision tree is best used when you not only look at the core questions, but also answer the sub-questions. There are, of course, situations where a quick decision is needed, right now. In that case, you can still look at the decision tree, just touching on the core questions, particularly the mission/values/strategy guidance.

In each of the remaining chapters we'll drill down into one or more of our core questions and review in depth each of the sub-questions.

Developing Your Own Decision Tree

Now that you've seen my suggestion for a decision tree, one option that is open to you is to simply adopt what you've read in the pages above. My recommendation, however, is to amend my decision tree to your specific issues, values, and situation. Perhaps you even need more than one decision tree: One for large strategic issues, and one for more mundane day-to-day issues. Or, you might want a tree that works for your board, and one (very similar, but probably more detailed) for your management team.

I do strongly urge you to read through the remainder of the book before developing your own decision tree. Why wait? Because each of the issues referred to in the core questions of the Smart Stewardship decision tree is discussed in much more detail in the remaining chapters of the book. Only after you read through these chapters will you be adequately prepared to consider which of my decision tree points to keep and which to amend or discard.

Whatever you decide to do, even if it is to adopt my decision tree without change (which I repeat, I do *not* recommend), there are three things to remember to do as you move forward.

☐ Be inclusive

Remember our Sixth Key to Smart Stewardship from Chapter 2? It was "You Have to Engage Everyone." No better place to start than here. Sit down with your management team first, and develop a rough decision tree. Run through one or two sample problems (see the following example) and amend the tree as needed. Next, go to your mid-level and line managers and run the idea of a decision tree by them. Show them your draft and ask for input. Again, try a mock problem with them. Give the line managers two or three days to consider the idea and meet with them again to get their additional input. Finally, it's time to go to the board and get their input as well.

 HANDS ON: While you could start with the board, and then move to the staff to get input, I don't recommend this sequence. Why? Because at its heart, the decision tree is a management issue, and thus one the staff has to be comfortable with first. The staff (as many as possible) should draft, test, amend, and improve the organizational decision tree first and bring it as a recommendation to the board. Can the board amend or ignore the idea? Sure. But if you stay close to the mission and values (that, I assume the board has adopted) there shouldn't be any major changes. And, since you want staff to use the tree on a daily or weekly basis, if it starts with them and isn't imposed by the board, your staff are more likely to use it willingly. ■

☐ Train, train, train

For many nonprofits, use of this kind of decision matrix will be something new. There will be misgivings, problems, and probably some pushback from staff who are unfamiliar with the idea. Obviously, having more people involved in the development of your decision tree will help with some of that concern, but the best way to get over it is to train yourself and others in how to use this new tool.

First, talk about the tool and the reasons for using it. Discuss what expectations are for its use: All decisions? Big decisions? Just for ideas brought up the management chain for approval? Then take people through a decision or two that are relevant to their level in the organization. For each group, start them with a small problem and move to a more difficult one. Thus for senior management you might start with a response to a Request for Proposal from a foundation, and then move to a more weighty issue like expanding services to an adjacent county. For mid-managers, you might start with an opportunity to develop a book club with their staff and then consider a decision to move to a new quality assurance system.

The idea is to develop the muscle memory needed to be comfortable and capable with the new decision tool.

 HANDS ON: It is crucial that the most senior staff are visibly involved with this training. You want to role model both learning and trying something that may be outside your comfort zone a bit. The message will be that we're innovating (look at this new decision model) and that our CEO/COO is learning right with us, trying something new, and making mistakes just like us. Be there, be visible, be fully engaged, and listen carefully to what's going on. ■

☐ Revisit your decision tree in six months

Time and practice (even after your training) will show you a lot about the use and effectiveness of the decision tree. Tell everyone on the staff to make notes as they use the matrix on ways that it can be improved. Make sure they tell you if they feel that using the tree stifles innovation, or encourages more discussion, or keeps people focused on the mission, or does something totally unexpected.

In six months, get a small team together (senior managers, board members, line managers) about how the decision tree worked and make formal suggestions on how to improve it.

One more time: A decision tree or matrix is an essential component of Smart Stewardship because it can enable better, more consistent, and mission-centric decisions throughout the organization.

As we move through the remainder of the book, you will see each of the core questions in my Smart Stewardship decision tree discussed at length. Remember what I said earlier: Even if you are chafing at the bit to develop a decision tree for your organization, read the rest of the book first. You'll be glad you did.

Recap

This chapter was all about our decision tree, why to use it, how to use it, and how to customize your decision tree using the one provided here as a starting point.

First, we looked at the basic question: Why use a decision tree? I showed you the big benefits of using such a tool, which included:

> More consistent decisions across the organization.
> The decision tree is a backup checklist for big or very fast decisions.
> The decision tree can help with delegation and reporting

Then, you got your first chance to examine the Smart Stewardship Decision Tree. You saw the seven core questions, which are placed in priority order within the Decision Tree and were:

- Mission, vision, strategy
- Capability
- Capacity
- Money
- Quality
- Analysis
- Consultation

I walked you through each of the core questions and their sub-questions in detail. We'll be coming back to these core and sub-questions in the remaining chapters of the book.

Finally, I showed you how to develop your own decision tree, using the Smart Stewardship decision tree as your starting point. As you develop your decision tree, I urged you to:

- ☐ Be inclusive
- ☐ Train, train, train, and
- ☐ Revisit your decision tree in six months

In our next chapter, we'll start our drill down with a detailed look at mission, values, and strategies.

Discussion Questions

1. Do we think that a decision format is a useful tool? Why or why not? Could it improve our delegation abilities?
2. Could we use Peter's decision tree in its current form? If not, how could we improve it?
3. How much training on our decision tree would our staff and board need? What about senior management? How do we make that happen?
4. Should we train, or just jump in and try to use the decision tree in real time? What kind of strategic questions could we practice on?
5. Is anyone aware of other peer organizations that are using such a method? How can we benefit from their experiences?

CHAPTER 4

Mission and Values

Chapter Thumbnail

Overview
Your Mission: Your Most Valuable Asset
Values: How You Do Your Mission
The Mission/Values Intersection
Creating a Culture around Your Mission and Values
Recap

Overview

As you make any decision, mission comes first. You'll no doubt remember what we discussed in Chapters 2 and 3; every decision you make must result in one or more of the following: more mission, better mission, more effective mission, more efficient mission. So, mission first, middle, last. After mission, you should consider your values, which are an often-overlooked component of any successful organization, but cannot be ignored or underused in any Smart Stewardship nonprofit.

In this chapter, we'll cover both mission and values in depth. We'll start where we should start: With your mission, and make sure you're using it in all the ways you should. Then we'll go to values, and talk about values creation and values-based operations.

After that groundwork, we'll look at how mission and values intersect in action, paying particular attention to one nonprofit's use of both mission and values in their management, staff benefits, and even the planning of their building.

Finally, I'll give you ways to create the culture you want around your mission and values. You can do so, so much more great mission if everyone in your organization is pointed in the same direction. Mission and values can be your organizational compass to make sure that everyone is pointed not only in the *same* direction, but more importantly, in the *right* direction.

Your Mission: Your Most Valuable Asset

You've already heard it a lot. You'll hear it more. You can't hear it enough.

Your mission is your most valuable asset. Let me repeat. Most. Valuable. Asset.

More valuable than your building, than your financial reserves, than your volunteers, and, yes, more valuable than your staff. Really? Yes. Because the mission is why the board and staff show up. The mission is why the building was built, why the reserves are in place, why you have a good reputation in the community. Your mission is the *why* of your organization.

Since it all starts with mission, it's appropriate that the first core question on the Smart Stewardship decision tree is about mission, and that the sub-questions begin with the outcome goal of more mission, better mission, more effective mission, and more efficient mission.

Let's drill down a bit more into why your mission is so important, and then think through how you can get more out of this, your most valuable asset. Your mission, if properly utilized, can be all of these things:

- A strategic and tactical touchstone
- A staff and volunteer recruiter
- A staff and volunteer motivator
- A fund-raising competitive advantage, and, oh yes,
- A compelling reason for the people who you serve to show up.

The question you should ask as a Smart Steward is: How do I get my mission to do all this? How do I turn that piece of paper on the wall into an organizational dynamo, and not just something our board adopted five (10, 15, 20?) years ago? How do I best use my most valuable asset?

Get the Mission You Want

You should start by making sure the mission you have is the mission you want. Is the mission accurate, concise, and inspiring? Let's look each of these in turn.

Accurate   This means that the mission statement describes what you truly do, particularly the where you do your work and who you help. While this sounds like a technical detail, it's important, particularly for nonprofits in the United States. If your mission statement does not correctly define the kinds of people and places you serve, the Internal Revenue Service (IRS) can and will find that your organization has Unrelated Business Income, and ding you for not filing your form 990-T.

This problem arises in many nonprofits over time. Say your nonprofit was formed in 1986 to help African-American teens in Cobb County, Georgia. Over the years, you've expanded to help people of many ethnicities and ages, and also expanded beyond the borders of Cobb County. Good for you, but if you haven't amended your mission (and filed that amendment with the IRS), the income you get for anything unrelated to African American teens in Cobb County is, well, unrelated.

Concise This means short and sweet. We live in a culture with very, very short attention spans. I liken this to the use of a television remote control; if I'm in the least bored or uninterested with what's on a channel, *click, click,* watch for a minute, nope, not interested, *click* . . . . Sound familiar? The basics are the same with your mission statement if it is long, drones on, or isn't quickly inspiring.

Let's say that you come up to me and I ask you what your organization does. You start to recite your mission statement. "*We help children* (I'm interested!) *and their families* (good!) *maximize their reintegration and unification skills* (huh?) *through a network of collaborating organizations* . . . *(click).* Even if I'm still standing in front of you, smiling, nodding, and looking you in the eye, mentally, I'm gone.

Concise is essential, but concise is hard. You have to boil down all the things you do to a concise description. And, in doing so, you'll almost certainly leave something someone on your board and staff cares deeply about unsaid, or at least not highlighted. Every phrase, noun, adjective, adverb, and most importantly verb you remove is painful. But it has to be done or you'll hear far too many *clicks.*

Inspiring As I've said, your mission is your key asset, so make it work for you. Turn it into your five-story elevator message so that people who hear the mission will want to know more rather than *click* away on you. Brevity is key, and the most difficult part of making something inspiring; we're all so proud and excited about our organizations we're sure that if we just keep talking (or writing) longer, people will get how cool our mission is. The trouble is that once that *click* occurs, you're done.

 FOR EXAMPLE: Goodwill Industries of North Georgia (GING) had a traditionally long and ponderous mission statement. In 2004 the senior staff decided to ask a representative group of staff (from many levels of the organization to come together and focus on
(*continued*)

(*continued*)

GING's mission and the way they used it. The mission statement at the time?

"The mission of Goodwill Industries of North Georgia is to build stronger communities by connecting people experiencing employment barriers to work."

There's nothing wrong with this statement, of course, but the work group concluded that it not only had jargon (what really *is* a "barrier to work"?), but was too long and not truly the focus of the organization. The work group thought through all their activities (including their thrift stores) and drilled down to the core. Their recommendation for a better mission statement?

"Our mission is to put people to work."

When you read the shorter mission, did you go "Huh? I thought Goodwill collected old clothes . . . ." If you did, that's exactly what GING wanted. Or if you thought "Cool, I'm all for more employment," or "Excellent, I have a friend who is out of work . . . " those reactions work too. Because what you almost certainly didn't do was . . . *click*. Later, you'll learn how GING used this accurate, concise, and inspiring mission statement to help focus its work and grow its mission in a remarkable fashion. But the focus and the growth started here, with the core mission. ■

Use Your Most Valuable Asset

Once you have your mission statement in the form you want, your next task is to put the mission to the best use possible. Remember, the idea here is to get the most from this asset, and that usually doesn't mean shouting it from the rooftops. Rather, it's better to have a much more focused use in ways that get to the key outcomes we discussed previously:

- A strategic and tactical touchstone
- A staff and volunteer recruiter
- A staff and volunteer motivator
- A fund-raising competitive advantage, and, oh yes,
- A reason for the people who you serve to show up.

Before I get into each of these, let me digress about telling mission stories. All nonprofits have powerful stories, most centered around the growth that people have made when services touch them. Whether a human services, arts, spiritual, community development, or other type of nonprofit, your organization almost always helps. And here's the key: That helping should turn into stories. People stories are the most effective way to communicate what your mission does.

And we're built to hear people stories. Look at the all-business *Wall Street Journal* sometime. Every day, on the front page, in the center column above the fold is a story about a person in the business or government world. A people story.

You have these stories by the dozen. I call them *Johnny and Jenny stories*: "Johnny was (really in trouble, unable to read, malnourished, homeless) when he walked in our door, and now he's doing great!", "Jenny and her family were (dysfunctional, out of a home, not making their rent payment) and now, look at them!" These are the stories that you want to find and tell to let people know about your mission.

 HANDS ON: Find your mission stories and talk about them all the time. At each board and staff meeting give a 90 second (really, just that long) Jenny or Johnny story to remind people about the mission. Remember this is particularly important for those on your staff who do not touch mission personally every day. NOTE: One great by-product of telling these stories is that it gives the board and staff a ready set of verbal shorthand to answer the common question from friends and family "What does your organization do?" "Well, we put people to work, but let me tell you a quick story about Jenny and her family . . . ." There won't be a *click* in that conversation.

Put mission stories on your web site and remember, video is cheap and the best way to tell these stories online. YouTube has brought the cost of making video way, way down. Like all things tech, you can use your younger staff and volunteers to get this done. Heck, you can go to your local high school National Honor Society advisor and ask him or her to give you a couple of students to help you. They almost always have video experience since they've done school projects in that format. ■

Find and tell your people stories. They are motivational gold.

Now that I've (hopefully) made that point sufficiently, let's return to our checklist of mission uses.

For **strategy and tactics**, do you use the mission in your decision making? Specifically? Does someone at the end of each staff and board meeting ask how the decisions made at that meeting improve the organization's mission capability? Did more than one or two people note that "This option has a better mission outcome . . . "? You can't talk about mission too much.

For **recruitment of staff and volunteers**, do you have your mission statement on your recruitment pages on your web site? Better yet, do you also have mission stories in video on your web site?

For **motivation of staff and volunteers**, tell the mission stories at every meeting, but make sure you offer the opportunity for different staff and volunteers to tell their own mission-based examples. Don't just have the meeting leader always tell the stories. Do, however, urge meeting leaders to be on the lookout for fresh mission-outcome stories all the time. Again, for board and staff who don't touch mission every day, this is a huge work benefit.

 FOR EXAMPLE: I was recently with some of the board members of a local Ronald McDonald House talking about board recruitment and retention, and best practices in governance. At one point during the meeting, I was talking about what motivates board members to serve, even what gets them to leave home or work and come to a board meeting. I asked those present what was the best part of their board service, the most satisfying, their best takeaway. I expected them to say things like "Helping the community," or "learning about how nonprofits work," or "giving back."

Not so much. Immediately after my question, one board member turned to the Executive and said, "The best part of my month is when you tell stories about the families that stay at the House during our board meetings!" Other board members almost giddily agreed. "That's the best!", "That's awesome!", "That's what it's all about!"   ∎

Yet again, tell your people stories.

In fund raising, short is better, getting to the point is key and the *click* comes way, way faster if you don't grab their attention. Make sure you use your mission and its resultant stories as effectively as you can (often in video) to make sure people know what their money is buying. Talk about mission outcomes, not just mission. Turn the mission statement around to give donors a chance to participate.

"At Goodwill, our mission is to put people to work. Last year, *X* people found work as a direct result of Goodwill's services. Your donation will help someone who is out of a job find meaningful employment. Help us put people to work."

You can't talk about mission too much. Most. Valuable. Asset.

Values: How You Do Your Mission

Now to values. As noted earlier, your mission is the why of your nonprofit and your values are the *how* of your nonprofit. Values can do much more than simply set the guidelines for staff and behavior; they can create and sustain the culture you want for your organization.

I like to think of values as an organizational magnet: They can simultaneously attract the people you want and repel the people you don't want for your team, both paid staff and volunteers. If you focus on, say, accountability as an organization-wide value for staff and board, and you do it front and center in recruitment, orientation, and evaluation, those people who prefer not to be held accountable for their actions or contributions will tend to go elsewhere. Similarly for common values I see such as quality, transparency, or respect. These values on a day-to-day basis will define your organization to the people you employ and the people you serve almost as much as your mission does.

But only if you lead them and live them, and here's the potential trap: You must lead values from the front. Or, to turn it around, never have a value you're not willing to lead.

 FOR EXAMPLE: In 2008, I was asked to perform a marketing audit and strategy session with a relatively large nonprofit in the Southwest. The chief executive officer (CEO) had been to one of my marketing training sessions a year before and was ready to show me what he had done in his nonprofit as a result of the training. We toured his programs and returned to his office, where he showed me the organizational mission and values prominently displayed on his wall. He told me that as part of the organization's refocusing on marketing, they had amended their values to add the term "Innovation" along with other values such as respect, forward leaning, and so on.

I asked the CEO how the values had been amended and, to make a long story short, he had done it the right way—very collaboratively, lots of time, effort, and participation throughout the organization. The CEO noted "We wanted to get to the idea of continuous improvement to keep cutting edge, and our values work groups decided that we all needed to be both flexible and innovative. Ultimately, we decided to focus on innovation throughout the organization. We now include innovation training, it's in our recruitment materials and a key part of every staff person's evaluation."

I was impressed. Later in the day, while the CEO left for a meeting offsite, I met with the senior management team. The team was great, very outgoing and enthusiastic about the organization and its mission. We discussed the marketing efforts and changes and, when the conversation waned a bit, I asked about the innovation initiative.

Conversation stopped, and everyone looked at the floor. Huh, I thought. "What?" I said. "Your CEO told me that your innovation
(continued)

(*continued*)

value was really driving change. Not true?" There was hemming and hawing and finally the COO looked up, cleared her throat and said, "You're going to talk to (the CEO) before you leave, right?" I said I was. "Well, the innovation value *is* good, and it *has* brought positive change. Everyone here supports it and it could be amazing, but . . . "

"But what?" I asked.

"Could you talk to the CEO about actually starting to use his email?"

Bam! There it was. The CEO who was touting innovation was not personally showing any flexibility or willingness to innovate himself. Remember, this was 2008, not 1988. Email was not exactly a new or cutting edge technology. And, while the value was working to a degree, it could have been turbocharged if only the CEO wasn't standing out in front of the building as a shining example of lack of innovation. ◼

 FOR EXAMPLE: Think about the often used value of *respect*. I see it regularly on value lists, and I think it's great—as long as it gets followed up on. It's closely related to the golden rule: Treat others as you'd like to be treated. So, if you have *respect* on your values list, do you respect the people you serve enough to regularly ask their opinion on how services should be provided? What about staff and volunteers? Do you respect them enough to value their intelligence and ideas?

Or take the example of downsizing. Times are hard, you have to cut a program or two and people, through no fault of their own, have to be laid off. Though not a human resources (HR) professional, I always think of layoff methodology choices fitting nicely inside a 2×2 grid like the following:

Legal		
Illegal		
	Right	Wrong

Obviously, when you need to lay someone off, you want to do it legally, but notice that within the Legal row, you have a choice—you can do the layoff *right* or *wrong*. What helps you decide what *right* is? Your values should. But let's look at the choice in more depth.

You can avoid treating the staff member who is about to be laid off (and who, remember, is innocent of wrongdoing—she's just the person who has to go) with any *respect* and have security notify her that she's been let go escort her out at 5:00 PM with no warning and no farewells to her friends, *or* you can treat her respectfully, tell her yourself, and ask her how she'd like to handle her departure. By the way, the first choice happened to a good friend of mine at a nonprofit about two years ago, and the organization's internal culture has yet to recover from the loss of faith within the remaining employees. ■

Create and Sustain the Culture You Want

Let's look at two common values and give you some questions to ask about how you would (or are) implement them.

Transparency Transparency is a terrific and increasingly common value. If you have it on your list, good for you. But ask yourself this question:

Is transparency only outside and not inside? If you feel you're transparent because you post your IRS 990, annual report, and your list of board and staff on your web site, that's just the start. You are not transparent if you don't let all your staff see your budget, or the minutes of your management team and board meetings, or your marketing plan, strategic plan, and so on. You can't have a value that is just for the people beyond the organization's doors.

Accountability Accountability is another terrific value. We all should be individually and collectively accountable for what we say and do. But this is risky, since we'll all fall short on occasion. So, if you have accountability on your list, do you post your organizational goals on your web site for all to see each year? How about the personal goals for the year of the CEO and management team? When you fall short of your goals do you note it?

 FOR EXAMPLE: I *love* local television weather forecasters who, each evening, review their prediction from the previous day and note how close they came to being right on target on temperature or precipitation. They're really out on the edge—thousands, even hundreds of thousands of people listen to the forecasters' predictions and make plans based on them. But these brave souls are willing to put their reputation on the line each day by reviewing what they predicted. By doing so, they build credibility with their audience, who doesn't expect them to be perfect, just trying harder. Good for them. ■

When you make a mistake, do you admit it and then move on? Or do you (intentionally or unintentionally) try to put forward an aura of perfection? If we do, are we really holding ourselves *accountable?* I think not.

Do you see what I mean? Values are great, but they have to be developed in a way that is both inclusive and constantly reinforced. Think about these steps as you consider developing and/or amending your organizational values.

Create or Amend Your Values List *Together*

If there is ever a time to be collaborative with your staff and volunteers, it's in the creation or amendment of your core values.

The worst thing you can do around value creation or amendment is to have an outside consultant create your values for you: Values created by a consultant aren't yours, they are the consultant's. Sounds obvious. But nearly as bad is to have a small group of the management team and board go off and come back from the mountaintop with the holy list of values. If you do that, the rest of the staff had nothing to do with the creation of the values and, while they might agree with the individual values listed, they don't have any ownership, and that, down the road, will be a problem.

Values need to be everyone's, not just the board's or the management team's. My suggestion is to assign a small, interdisciplinary team from all levels of your organization to develop your initial list, with examples of how those values play out in the real world, and how your organization may *not* be living by the value now (this is actually more common than you might expect). Then float the values for comments, and have some group meetings around the upcoming suggestions.

Make Your Values Analog, Not Digital

If you make your values too specific, you don't leave room for discussion, and discussion is crucial around values. My shorthand for this is to make your values analog, not digital. An analog watch or clock can be read as "11:52" *or* "a little before noon" *or* "roughly 10 before 12." The digital timepiece says 11:52.

Now, you might be asking, "Don't you *want* values that are very specific? Don't you *want* to give people the most guidance possible?" For rules and policies, yes. For values, no, and here's why. You want your values to be guidance, but also discussion/argument starters, because that's what builds common understanding and, ultimately, your culture. You want discussion because you want people to grow within the values and understand how to interpret them on their own, without you looking over their shoulder.

FOR EXAMPLE: Every reader knows of Google, the online search giant. Most of us use one or more of their tools every day. But do you know their core value? There's only one, and it's guided the business since its beginnings. And, it's only three words, "Don't be evil."

That's it, and it's totally analog. I've met and talked to people fairly high up in the food chain at Google and to a person, they say that people in the company argue about this value *all the time*. Each new application or service brings out people within the firm who feel that it might have the potential to "be evil," either in the short or long term." "Some of the battles are epic," one manager told me, "but they all wrap around this value. It's awesome and it's made us rethink pretty much everything we do." ■

That's exactly what you want to have happen in your organization. As decisions are made, you want people to ask whether you can implement it with *respect*, or accountability, and then specifically how. Different perspectives are key, thus my urging for widely inclusive collaboration. Remember, analog, not digital.

Talk about What Your Values Mean on the Ground

Speaking of interpretation and different perspectives, now is the time to discuss what each suggested value will mean in the real world, on the ground every day. It's nice and easy and safe to write the word *respect* on the flip chart when you're developing your organizational values, but what does that mean? We've already seen my challenge questions for you on this value and others. But here's a short list of things I've heard staff and board members of nonprofits say the word *respect* means to them:

"Respect means that every manager should say please and thank you to each of their staff when they ask for something to be done."

"Respect means that when I ask for time off (which I almost never do), management respects my privacy and doesn't ask why I need the time off."

"Respect for our clients means offering them a chance to pay for services even though they don't have to."

"Respect means not yelling."

"Respect means that older workers should not blow off younger workers' ideas."

"Respect should not be assumed. It should be earned."

I suspect when you read that list of reactions there was at least one that made you go "Huh." All of these, as well as asking everyone's opinion, or laying people off differently, are the ripples that occur when you throw the *respect* stone in the pond. The key is that you want to see the ripples sooner rather than later, so have the discussion now. Only keep the values you can live with.

Proclaim Your Values

Once you have your values agreed to and adopted by the board, you need to start the accountability train by posting the values clearly online, giving a copy to each staff person, volunteer, and service recipient and posting them visibly throughout your organization.

 HANDS ON: Remember, if you are going to use your values to shape your culture, you have to start with staff and volunteer recruitment. On the "Careers" page of your web site, you should have the mission and the values front and center. Same for orientation for those who get hired, and for evaluations for everyone. Here is a sample of how a few values could look on the career page:

Our Values

> *Respect:* We respect ourselves, each other, and our community, but most importantly, the people we serve. If you want to work in a place where your opinion counts, we're a great place to be, and you'll hear "please" and "thank you" a lot if you work here.
>
> *Accountability:* We hold ourselves and each other accountable every day. We strive to say what we mean and mean what we say. If you want to work in a "No whining" and "No excuses" zone, we'd love to have you join us.
>
> *Transparency:* We feel we work for the community and thus everything we do should be visible to the community. This also means that inside the organization, we're open and sharing with information. We try hard to avoid secrecy and dark corners.

While most organizations would have more values, and certainly a different spin on what they mean, this gives you an idea of how to actualize the values in your recruitment. ■

Welcome Values-Based Criticism

No matter how much conversation and discussion you have, a week after you adopt your values, someone will take a shot at you, on a personal or organizational level, suggesting that you've violated a key value. I promise, this *will* happen. Be like the people at Google and embrace the discussion. And, remember that how you, as the leader, handle the first critique is *crucial*. If you ignore it, or blow it off, all the hard work you've put in will be for naught.

Once that initial discussion is behind you, go further. Note to all staff and volunteers that the values are not much help if they are just words on the wall. Tell everyone that they should hold each other (and you) accountable based on the values, and that you look forward to their ideas and input.

So now you know how important organizational values are to a non-profit that wants to practice Smart Stewardship. You understand that values shape your behavior and your culture, and that you need values that are analog and not just digital. Hopefully, your staff and volunteers will help you shape your organizational decisions in a way that both supports your mission and respects your values. That's what I call the mission/values intersection and it's our next subject of discussion.

The Mission/Values Intersection

How do you put mission and values into action? What's the trick in not letting the enthusiasm of mission and values creation or update wane away? How do you, in the trendy term actualize the mission and values?

You do that where they meet—at the mission/values intersection. Where is that intersection. On the ground, at the front lines, in your decisions and actions every day. Smart Stewards know (or learn quickly) that if their actions don't reflect their values or support their mission, they've lost a key edge, an extra boost to all their resources. But if they do make sure that their decisions reflect the values, they can supercharge their organization, and this becomes what economists call a virtuous loop. Because you focus on values-based actions, people (who came to your organization because of the mission and values) are happier. They do better work, which makes the community happier with you and you (in most economies) get more work, make more values-based decisions, and so on.

There's a second loop as well. If you, the leader, are up front about the fact that values matter in your decision making and you discuss it regularly and openly, others will follow your example—and the virtuous cycle begins again—without your being present. You build a culture based on mission and values.

Peckham Values

Peckham's organizational values permeate everything they do, and most visibly, had major impact on their headquarters building. I've had the opportunity to see the building and regularly describe it to friends and colleagues as the only values-based building I've ever seen.

As background, here are the Peckham values: *Peckham believes in empowering the individual to self-advocate in pursuit of their vocational goals. Every person, whether client or employee, is encouraged to reach for their potential while embracing the values at the heart of Peckham: excel, collaborate, speak with integrity, exceed expectations, and embrace diversity. This empowerment leads to innovation in programs, products, and processes.*

The value of collaboration is particularly visible, as Peckham includes everyone in planning and innovation. Town meetings with all staff are held regularly, and input from those meetings is credited with major new initiatives and directions in contracting, including adding more high-tech jobs for persons with severe disabilities.

Values are also key in recruitment. Staff are first screened for their values, not their experience with people with disabilities. If their values fit with Peckham's, they're hired, and trained in the best practices of working with persons with disabilities. "We're more concerned about hiring a person who will fit, who understands our mission and values—we can train them to do the job." "A good supervisor somewhere else may not be a good supervisor here if they don't get our focus on people first over process."

Lakeview Values

When Mark, Lakeview's new senior pastor, arrived, there was much anticipation about how he would handle himself. What would he do differently than his recently retired predecessor? What would he not change?

On the first Sunday Mark preached, he changed a key tradition at the church: Where the pastor sat prior to his sermon. Mark's predecessor had always sat up on the stage, facing the parishioners. On Mark's first Sunday preaching, there was no chair on stage. After the music, introductions, announcements, offering, and the like, it was time for Mark to preach, and he stood up—in the front row of the church—and walked up to the stage.

Mark was leading by example one of the values he felt important: That the preacher is a *member* of the congregation, not above them.

"I was stunned by what Mark did," said a 30-year member of the church, " . . . and I loved it. It embodied the way our church should be."

Will having values that you talk about all the time always work? Of course not. It's not just what you say, it's what you do. On the good side of things, Lakeview's pastor embodied his values personally. Then, there's the dark side.

Most readers know the story of Enron, the huge energy-trading company that was also a huge scam on the shareholders. Enron collapsed in late

2001, but during its boom years, was reporting rapid (but false) growth to Wall Street, Congress, and the press. One of the tools that Ken Lay, the chairman of Enron, used was the "Enron Values," which he touted every chance he got. Here they are:

Respect: *We will treat others as we would like to be treated. We do not tolerate abusive or disrespectful treatment.*

Integrity: *We work with customers and prospects openly and sincerely. When we say we will do something we will do it. When we say we cannot or will not do something then we won't do it.*

Communication: *We have an obligation to communicate. Here, we take the time to talk to each other . . . and to listen. We believe that information is meant to move and that information moves people.*

Excellence: *We are satisfied with nothing less than the very best in everything we do. We will continue to raise the bar for everyone. The great fun here will be for all of us to discover just how good we can really be.*

Of course, no one talked about these values in any way, shape, or form inside the company; it was basically an organization without any internal values at all, an ethical and moral free for all.

The point here is that developing mission and values statements is great (and, if you do it collaboratively, can garner a huge team-building benefit), but if they are just words on the wall, they're *worse than nothing*. Remember, your staff looks at your list of values either as an inspiration (if actualized every day) or as a sham. As a leader, your actions will decide whether or not your mission/values intersection will help your organization by creating a virtuous cycle of mission, or set it back buried under a landslide of cynicism.

Creating a Culture around Your Mission and Values

We've already discussed a number of ways that you can actualize your mission and, on a day-to-day level, your values. Even so, I need to take this space to reiterate how important this is in creating your organizational culture.

As John Maxwell, the author of many great leadership books, says; "If you don't like the actions of the people you've hired, look to yourself first." What Maxwell is saying is that people tend to group with people who are like them, who have similar interests, passions, and values. Most of us tend to avoid people who have significantly different priorities or values. We certainly don't seek them out. As I said earlier, values are like a magnet—they either attract or repel you.

> **FOR EXAMPLE:** A few years back, my eldest son was hired by a firm that was in a business that looked very interesting and cutting edge. The product supported one of Ben's values, and he was pleased to get an interview, then a second interview, then a third and a job offer. After each visit, he and I talked, and it was clear he had concerns about the people in the firm, but couldn't put his finger on what was bothering him. Ben chalked up his worries to the fact that the company's focus kept rapidly changing and nothing more. He accepted the job offer.
>
> Two weeks after he started, he resigned. Once he had been inside the company, he had quickly realized that his values did not align at all with the company's leadership. Ben confronted his employers with his concerns, and was, to say the least, unsatisfied with their reaction and response. He left (in the teeth of a recession) and never looked back. ■

Not everyone is as lucky as Ben was, with a skillset that was very much in demand and no serious immediate financial obligations such as a mortgage or a family to feed. Others are not so lucky, and if they stay in a situation where their values are in conflict with the norm, they'll be miserable . . . and it will show in their work.

Building (or, if you're new in your leadership position, reshaping) a culture takes time, like the well-worn example of turning the Titanic. But it will not happen at all if you don't make it intentional. You, as the leader, have to go after the change you want, and since cultures are really built around shared values and beliefs, you should start there.

Here are the steps I suggest you take:

- Make sure you have the mission you want.
    - Go back to the first section in this chapter and review your mission. Is it *click*-proof? If not, change it, and do this as collaboratively as possible. Remember to have your board adopt the change and to notify the IRS of the new charitable purpose.
- Create or update your values.
    - Do this collaboratively, with as many people as possible. Remember to talk through the meaning of the values on the ground. Have more meetings with more staff on your values than you've ever had on any organizational issue. This alone will highlight their importance.
- Proclaim your mission and values.
    - Put the updated mission and values everywhere you can, on the walls, on people's business cards, on the screen savers on people's

computers. Make them front and center on many parts of your web site.

- Use the values magnet
  - Attract or repel people with your values, by putting them front and center in recruitment, orientation, and evaluation. Make them part of your regular compliments for people who take actions that are value laden. Create employee awards, one for each value. Add the values (and ways for the organization to be more value laden) to your staff satisfaction survey. Six months after you establish and proclaim your values, hold a few focus groups with an outside facilitator to get feedback on how people feel about the values and how the organization can improve. Repeat this exercise a year later.
- Talk about values in every meeting of the board, committees, and staff.
  - Make sure to ask people how their decisions support the values, and expect them to ask, even challenge, you in return.

Most importantly when you, singular, or you, collectively, make a values error, admit it, apologize, and get back at it.

One final word on this. It is very likely that some of your staff or volunteers (or both) will mock the idea of developing and living by values. Ignore them—they're the ones being repelled by your values magnet, and if you keep at it long enough, they'll either leave or be silenced by peer pressure. Do *not* waste your time trying to change their minds.

Others, though, may feel like you're preaching, or criticizing their personal values. This is more often the case when you, the leader, are new. People will sometimes wrongly assume that you're implying that the organization's values before you arrived were poor. These people need to be assured, by you directly, that no criticism is intended, that you're not saying that what they did was wrong, but rather working to do it even better for the people you serve. Don't ignore these folks, talk with them individually and personally.

Mission and values are the why and the how of your nonprofit. If you get them right, if you lead from the front, if you build your culture around them, then you've taken the most important two steps in becoming a Smart Steward. Other key decisions and actions must follow, but if you don't get this part right, you'll never be truly and completely successful in delivering the best mission to the people you serve.

Recap

In this chapter, we took on the two key foundations of your nonprofit, and thus of your decision making: your mission and your values. I told you that your mission is not only the why of your organization, but also its most valuable asset, one that you need to get the most out of each day. We reviewed the ways your mission can be useful, which included being:

- A strategic and tactical touchstone
- A staff and volunteer recruiter
- A staff and volunteer motivator
- A fund-raising competitive advantage, and, oh yes,
- A reason for the people who you serve to show up.

I urged you to turn your mission into people stories and share those as much as possible.

Then, we turned to your values, which are the *how* of the way you do mission. We discussed the fact that your values help create your culture, act as a magnet—either attracting or repelling staff and volunteers—and we looked at some ways to collaboratively create (and amend) your values to put them to the best effect.

I suggested ways to better use your values, including in staff recruitment, orientation, and evaluation, as well as in decision-making, double-checking to make sure your actions in pursuit of mission don't violate your values.

Most importantly, we talked about the fact that values have to be led from the front, and that there's a trap here for managers; if you espouse a certain value to your staff but aren't willing to live it yourself, you're in big trouble and so, ultimately, is your organization.

Next we turned to the mission-values intersection, which is where, to use the old phrase, the rubber hits the road. We looked at Peckham Industries and Lakeview Christian as wonderful examples of this intersection.

Finally, we examined how to create an organizational culture around your mission and values, developing a high satisfaction environment for staff and volunteers that feeds on the good you do and the way it's done.

Now you know the touchstones of better decision making and where the best, most mission-rich decisions start: with your mission and values. Now, and only now, are you are ready to go to the next step in our Smart Stewardship decision tree, which examines your nonprofit's capability and capacity. Those are interesting and essential components of any decision, but if you skip the mission and values, it will all be for naught. Even if you have lots of capacity and tons of capability, without your mission and values, you'll just be all dressed up with no place to go.

Mission first, then values, then everything else.

Discussion Questions

1. How recently have we looked at our mission statement? Does it really focus on what we do? Does it meet Peter's *click* test?
2. Let's list 10 people stories that are mission outcomes. How can we hone these into *short* stories to share?
3. What are our values? How were these values developed? Once we have our mission refined, what's the best way for us to develop values our staff and board can embrace?
4. Let's think about ways that our on-the-ground actions *do* as well as the ways that they *don't* embody our mission or our values. What can we learn from Peckham's experience?
5. How can we be better about using our mission and values to create a more satisfying culture for everyone?

CHAPTER 5

Understanding Capability and Capacity

Chapter Thumbnail

Overview

Our next checkpoint on the Smart Stewardship decision tree is capability and capacity. Does your organization have enough of both to handle the results of your decision? If you're considering downsizing, what will the effects be on both your capacity and your capabilities.

That's what we'll examine in this chapter. First, we'll look at capability by immediately raising the bar from capable to competent. You need to discover what your core competencies are and carefully nurture them. You also need to figure out what you things you are not truly good at, and either ramp them up, or get out of that service or task. I'll show you how.

Next, we'll examine the method of looking down the road and see what core competencies your nonprofit will need in the next few years, and how to get started on improving in those areas. You may have to add a core value, hire a different skill set, or get volunteers to fill holes in certain areas. This is crucial to keeping your status as Smart Stewards.

Then we'll turn to capacity, which not only means people and physical space, but also the often ignored back-office tasks like tech and human resources, as well one other resource that we say we never have enough of, but always treat as limitless when taking on new tasks: time. I'll show you how to think through your current capacity and then how to decide when to add capacity incrementally. Do you ramp up before the shortages are present, or after they show their ugly heads? Not as easy a choice as it might seem, and we'll look at this issue in depth.

Finally, I'll give you a capacity checklist as a starting point, one that you can add to and edit as you work your way through the decision process. There may be some things you haven't thought of as resources that you need to make sure you consider, as well as some current resources that you may want to discard or outsource. We'll examine those choices as well.

By the end of this chapter, you'll have a much better idea of how to evaluate your competencies and your capacity in a way that will help assure that the decisions you make are within your reach, that your quality of service can remain high, and that you stage growth or downsizing in a realistic way.

Core Competencies: What Is Your Organization Really Good At?

Capabilities are different than competencies. Just because we are capable of something does not necessarily mean we are really good at it.

 FOR EXAMPLE: Until I had a hip replacement in 2011, I was a runner, logging anywhere from 700 to 1,500 miles a year for more than 30 years. I ran marathons, half-marathons, innumerable 10k and 5k races, and a couple of dozen triathlons. I could run.

But I could never run fast. I was regularly in the slowest quartile of any large run in which I participated. I even had an article published in *Triathlete Magazine* titled "The View From the Back of the Pack." I was capable of running, I really enjoyed it, it was something I spent a great deal of time and effort doing, but I was never *great* at it. I had the capability to run, and run a long way, but it was not a *core competence.* ■

The same issue exists in many nonprofits. We have services we've done forever, ones that we've put tons of time and money into. In some cases these services are a key part of our organizational identity and traditions. But do we provide them *really* well? Or, like many organizations, have they gotten stale, or underfunded, or placed on the back burner and are now really provided *adequately* and not superbly.

The first takeaway here is that **the people you serve deserve to be served better than just adequately**. I know there are always financial tensions and tradeoffs, and we'll discuss them in a minute, but let's agree that we shouldn't start with settling for adequate.

My second admonition relates to your Smart Stewardship decision making.

If you're considering expanding as a policy, find out what you're really good at—and do more of that. Don't just chase available funds to do more of what you only do adequately. On the flip side, if you're thinking of downsizing, start by casting off the stuff where you're only adequate.

FOR EXAMPLE: A human services nonprofit in the part of the world known as Oceana had provided what is termed congregate housing (units of 8 to 10 residents) for people with serious mental illness for more than 25 years. They also provided small group homes, employment, counseling, and transportation services, but the core of their identity (and income) was in the congregate housing area. Over the years as standards rose, funding stayed the same. Like many providers in other parts of the world, the organization struggled with low pay (and resulting high staff turnover), the difficulty in adapting to new record-keeping demands, and attaining high marks for quality.

Finally, the board and staff went on a retreat to examine all of the organization's services, and to think through how to improve all of them. It quickly became apparent that the congregate housing was the quality laggard, and that, with current funding streams, there was no viable way of improving them to the standards that the board and staff felt comfortable with.

After much consideration and significant thought, the nonprofit decided to get out of the congregate housing market. They found another nonprofit to take over the units, transferred the staff that they could, and walked away from the service. As well as from 35 percent of their total organizational revenue and 40 percent of their annual profits. Not an easy decision, but one I applaud. ▪

I've thrown around the term core competence a lot. Exactly what is a core competence? The concept was first introduced by C. K. Prahalad and Gary Hamel in their 1990 book *The Core Competence of the Corporation*. Prahalad and Hamel describe core competence as something that an organization can do well that meets three conditions:

1. It provides consumer benefits;
2. It is not easy for competitors to imitate;
3. It can be leveraged widely to many products and markets.

So, for example, if a particular nonprofit is really good at on-line fund-raising (as evidenced by the fact that they make a lot of net revenue doing it) such a competency would benefit the people they serve by providing net funds for services. But can the technical and marketing know-how be leveraged for other things throughout the nonprofit? Perhaps. What about the competitive advantage? Yet another question to be answered.

Since so many nonprofits do not really compete for services (they have been granted essential geographic monopolies by funders), I think that particular criteria is a bit off center for our field. So, I suggest that you look at the following criteria for your evaluation of core competence inside your nonprofit:

1. Do we have objective evidence (accreditation or outcome measures, for example) that our skill in this area is exceptional?
2. Can this core skill be used/transferred across our organization?
3. Do we have highly educated and experienced people leading in this area of our organization?
4. Does this competence make us more mission capable?

Obviously, there are no numerical ratings here, your self-examination will include some objective measures (accreditation, for example) and some subjective ones (how experienced do your people need to be?). But I've found these criteria work as realistic discussion starters within nonprofits and can lead to more clear-eyed reviews of what an organization excels at and what it does not.

But the discussions are still hard, and your people will defend their area of work for the very human reason of not wanting to feel that they are/were part of a service or support area that was either poorly managed or even just adequate. Expect that kind of pushback.

Sometimes establishing what your core competencies are requires you to distill all the things you do down to the essence of what makes your organization great.

 FOR EXAMPLE: In the late 1990s I had the opportunity to work with an amazing nonprofit based in Quincy, Illinois, named Chaddock. Chaddock provides residential treatment for youth from ages 8 to 21 on their campus, and have some of the best outcomes with very troubled kids of anywhere in the nation.

During my time with them, one of the things we did was to try to drill down into their core competencies. A large group of staff met repeatedly, walking through each service and support function, trying to establish where the organization was great, where it was good, and where it wasn't.

It was a lot of work and very frustrating to the employees, as some of them felt their areas of work were getting unfairly criticized. We bogged down in one meeting and, in order to regain some momentum, I asked everyone to put their pens and paper down, to sit back and close their eyes and to think about Chaddock as a whole, not as each individual service. I asked them to think about describing Chaddock in the best way they could to their best friend.

There was silence (and, I suspect, some napping going on) for a few minutes, then one manager said "You know, the most important thing we're good at is *we're really good with difficult kids*. All of us." There was general agreement, and then someone hit the nail on the head. She said, "It's more than just being really good with difficult kids. We're really good with *the most difficult* kids. *That's* us."

And it was true. The core competence of *being really good with the most difficult kids* was supported by Chaddock's outcome measures, by their accreditation, by their reputation. Being good with the most difficult kids also was something they shared and expected throughout the organization; it was important for the janitors to be good with those kids just as much as the therapists or house parents—a true core competence. ■

Start with Data and Accreditation

My suggestion is to start with discussions internally using my criteria above. Pretty quickly, though, your staff and board will begin to look for outside comparisons, what are commonly called best practices, wanting to compare your organization to others in your field. When the data is there, this is great. In Chaddock's case there was increasingly good comparative data on long-term results with their residents compared with other organizations like them both in Illinois and the Midwest. Their staff and board could say with confidence that their program worked. The data allowed for that and can help you if it's being collected. When there's not a central data repository, when your funder or funders don't have or reimburse for data collection and analysis, this gets harder.

Which is why so many nonprofit organizations (and their funders) turn to accreditation to fill the gap. Accreditation is usually a rigorous review of a variety of services, management and governance practices, and a financial review, performed by a national body that uses standards created by the field. Sometimes a national trade association will provide an accreditation, sometimes it's an independent nonprofit.

FOR EXAMPLE: A physician graduates from medical school and does her residency in her specialty. Let's say she's a family practitioner in the United States, and she wants to be seen as one of the best in her field; she'll apply for the status Degree of Fellow of the American Academy of Family Practitioners. ■

 FOR EXAMPLE: A nonprofit that provides services to people with developmental disabilities may well apply for accreditation from the Commission on Accreditation of Rehabilitation Facilities (CARF). In truth, the nonprofit may not have the choice: Being accredited by CARF is more and more a prerequisite to receive funding from state government or foundations. CARF accreditation is expensive, time-consuming, nerve-wracking, and, in the words of every chief executive officer (CEO) I know who's gone through it, absolutely worth it. "We can never take our eye off the ball. Even when we get a three-year accreditation (and thus don't have to go through the process again for 36 months) we know it's coming and keep up with best practices." ■

 FOR EXAMPLE: Nearly every hospital in the United States is accredited by the Joint Commission on the Accreditation of Hospitals (JCAH). Again an expensive and rigorous process, it's well worth it from the patients' point of view. If I discovered that a hospital near me was not JCAH accredited, I'd avoid it like the plague. Why take the chance? ■

 HANDS ON: If your organization does have accreditation (or seeks it after reading this), use the process to help you identify your core areas of expertise. Talk to your surveyors (the people who come to your organization to review your files, talk to staff, etc.) about their experiences elsewhere. See how you stand up to the field. ■

 HANDS ON: Once you have your accreditation, make sure your community knows. Proclaim your accomplishment on your web site, on the homepage, the donations page, the staff and volunteer recruitment page, along with a brief description of what the importance of the accreditation is; "We're CARF Accredited" is unintelligible jargon to most people. ■

Check with Your Customers

Accreditation and data comparisons from other agencies are terrific, if they exist for your field of service. Start there. In some cases, there won't be the information you need, or the accrediting body will be too expensive or not available. In either case, the next step is to go with data you do have, from your customer/clients/patients/patrons.

You should be collecting some kind of customer satisfaction information, and if you're not, now's a great time to start. There is a great deal of information on this kind of asking in my book *Mission-Based Marketing Third Edition* also published by John Wiley and Sons. One survey is, of course, not enough. You need to do repeated asking over time to make sure that your services do not decline un-noticed by staff and management. Trust me your customers, the people you serve, will notice and tell you. So ask, ask regularly, and pay attention to the answers.

Finally, Take a Collaborative Vote

Exhibit 5.1 shows a sample competency evaluation grid for a nonprofit that provides a range of arts services to children and teenagers. Some of the services are named by their nickname, which is fine; this is really an internal document. The key here is not the names of the services across the column heads, but rather the evaluation criteria along the left side. Take a look, and as you do, think about what criteria you'd add, change, or delete.

This grid, actually used by a youth art program a few years back, was designed around a board and staff examination to decide if each program was worth expanding. In the end, one program was abandoned, two were grown.

EXHIBIT 5.1 Sample Competency Evaluation Grid

	K-3 Art Experience	Art After School	Creative Zone	Steppin' Up
Accredited?				
Repeat customers?				
Awards?				
Experience of teachers?				
Education level of teachers?				
Do we track alumni?				
Clear goals for program?				
Student satisfaction				
What's the core competence here?				
Comments				

The key here is twofold: First, put down what you think is important in the criteria column. For example, it was important to the nonprofit whether families signed their children up over and over (repeat customers), particularly in the Creative Zone and Steppin' Up programs, since those were targeted at kids with a diagnosis of attention deficit hyperactivity disorder (ADHD). The criteria also drove the organization to start collecting data on student satisfaction and gave teachers a clear indication that experience and education were important.

Most importantly, though, is to *not* limit the distribution of this evaluation tool to just the CEO or key management team. Let more people have input. Everyone has an opinion, and by letting the people in one program evaluate all the programs, you get a better outcome and better decisions. If you don't believe me, read James Surowiecki's wonderful book *The Wisdom of Crowds* on group decision making. Surowiecki's premise (backed up by data) is that a group of one hundred randomly selected individuals will almost always make a better decision than two experts. I suspect this is not true for neurosurgery, but you get the idea.

Ask more. Get input from throughout the organization. Find out what the consensus is on what you're best at, compare that to any data you have, and establish your core competencies. Then, work hard to keep them. Best practices are always a moving target.

Choosing Core Competencies Going Forward

Once you go through the evaluation of your current core competencies, you can then look at two other competency issues; what you are now doing that did not make the cut into core competence, and what you are not yet doing that you need to be incredibly good at down the road.

You can get some guidance in this area by referring to your strategic plan and, if you don't have a plan, this is an excellent reason to do one. Planning requires you to look out and see what's coming, and what's coming may require you to develop some new competencies. Let's look at two competencies I think pretty much every nonprofit needs to have going forward Some of your organizations already are there, some . . . not so much.

Story Telling

I know, most readers are not managing a preschool, and thus you may think this is not for you, but I believe it's one of the key competencies of successful nonprofits from here on out. Think back to our discussion about the power of mission (Johnny and Jenny) stories in Chapter 4. People love stories about people, and it's the most powerful way to describe what your mission really does. That's great, and you have lots of stories, but the way you frame and tell the story is key.

All of us have been enraptured by a good storyteller. And, we've all been bored by someone who may have a great story to tell, but can't stay on track, doesn't keep their storytelling reasonably focused, goes off track, and so on.

While I admonished you to do some of your storytelling on video on your web site, the most powerful and common stories will be told orally, from you to a patron, from your staff to a friend, from your board members to someone in the community.

Get good at this, and then find a story-telling leader in the organization who both shows how to tell a story the most effective way, and then helps others by putting the key facts about your Johnny and Jenny stories in print or online as a resource for your staff and board. There are lots of books and videos (particularly on YouTube) regarding how to ramp up your storytelling. Check them out.

Embracing Technology

In my book *Mission-Based Management, Third Edition,* I list the 10 key characteristics of successful nonprofits. One of those is "Embracing Technology for Mission." Not *accepting* technology, *putting up with* technology, *using* technology, or *exploiting* technology, but rather *embracing* technology for mission. If you are a baby boomer like me, this may be a stretch, since you're happy just to read your email without the computer locking up and you don't get Facebook or Twitter. That's okay for you, but not for the organization. Nonprofits who don't embrace technology for mission run the risk, if not likelihood, of losing two entire generations of staff, volunteers, donors, and people to serve. Strategically, I don't think there is any other way to go than to get really, really good at using technology for mission, whether it be social networks, mobile apps, or whatever comes down the road. And, you may already have the expertise on hand—it's much more likely that your younger staff and volunteers get this than people my age. Your job as a leader is to recognize the need for tech as a core competence and cut the experts loose.

I know there are other competencies your organization needs to focus on, and now you have the skills to go sniff them out, and get the task of getting good on your organizational to-do list.

Now that we have the competence issue on track, let's look at the second part of the Smart Stewardship decision tree, one that often gets overlooked in the rush to do mission.

Capacity: Measuring Your Ability to Grow Your Mission

Your organization may well be capable, competent, or even world class at a function or service, but if you outstrip your capacity, your skills take a back seat and you can't fulfill your mission goals.

 FOR EXAMPLE: For 25 years, I held a private pilot's license. I flew a lot, kept up my proficiency ratings rigorously, and was what's termed *instrument rated,* meaning I could fly in or above clouds, without being able to see the ground, or even five feet in front of the windscreen. My annual reviews were always good, and I got many compliments from instructors. I was a competent pilot.

But I was not, ever, a cocky pilot. My father-in-law was a combat veteran, who flew bombers over Germany during World War Two. He was thrilled when I was getting my pilot's training, and wanted to fly with me (read: check out the guy who was going to fly his daughter and grandchildren around) soon after I got my license. When he pronounced me competent, I was appreciative, but always remembered his admonition: *"There are old pilots, and there are bold pilots, but there are no old, bold pilots."*

So, one day, perhaps 15 years after I received my wings, this competent, but never bold, pilot flew two colleagues from central Illinois over to Iowa for the day. We took a four-seater, single-engine plane in which I had logged hundreds of hours. My friends were bidding on some work in stained glass restoration. We flew to Iowa, they took off for their meeting, and I hung out and did work I'd brought along in the pilot's lounge. Four hours later they returned . . . carrying a 175-pound piece of stained glass in a wooden crate. Uh oh.

All aircraft have limits, called the plane's flight envelope (this is where the term "push the envelope" comes from; it's what test pilots do every day). If you're too heavy, you obviously can't take off, but the weight limit is also a function of altitude, temperature, length of the runway, and, most importantly, the balance of the aircraft. Weight and balance are crucial, and even more so in smaller planes.

All this was going through my head as I saw this dense 175 pounds coming toward me. One of my friends was a big guy to start with, as am I. It was a hot day (which reduces your capability to take off heavy), and I knew we just couldn't throw the glass in the back of the plane where luggage went—the weight and balance would be off.

My friends were eager to leave. They had other appointments. I wanted to keep them happy, but I stood looking at the glass and said,

"I gotta do a bunch of calculations. We may not be able to take off. You guys go weigh the glass, weigh yourselves (there was a scale in the lounge for just this purpose), and come tell me what the numbers are. Then, see if you can get the glass, along with Steve (the big guy), in the back seat. I'm pretty sure we'll need to keep this out of the luggage storage."

"Why?" they asked.

"Let me go figure for a minute."

I went inside to the pilot's lounge, got out my calculator and the flight envelope information and did my calculations. *If* the runway was long enough and *if* we took off before it got to be 90 degrees, we'd be fine, at least according to my numbers. But it was close, so I called the aircraft manufacturer and conferred with them, giving our weights and the other situational data. All on the phone agreed we could take off, but the manufacturer's rep suggested I pump out some of my fuel first just to be safe. I'd still have plenty left over, and it was a good idea.

So, after losing some fuel weight, we loaded up, went to the long runway, took off and climbed . . . veeerrryyyy slowly. We were right at the limits of the plane's capacity. Near, but not at, the edge of the envelope. Once airborne, we were fine and completed the trip without incident. ■

The point of this story is that while we had competence, we were at the limits of our capacity. My friends were ready to go (think of this as the pressure you get when you or your staff are ready to do mission) and I wanted to acquiesce. But I needed to stop and think before we jumped off, to make sure our capacity, in all its complexity, was not exceeded.

The important thing to remember is that when mission opportunities present themselves, nonprofit staff and board tend to say yes. We look at the obvious: "We have this skill," or "We're already doing that, doing more of it is easy," or "That's *such* a high need in our community, let's do it!," and forget the parts of the organization that are out of sight: human resources (HR), information technology (IT), finance, and other key parts of our organization. Most commonly, we underestimate the cost of a new program in that absolutely limited resource, time. Isn't it interesting that we all say we don't have enough time, yet repeatedly add new tasks or responsibilities to our own and our management teams' portfolio and underestimate how much time it will take?

Let's look at where you are now, and then examine the kinds of capacity you should be considering in your decision making.

Are You Over Capacity Already?

Before you even think about growing more, as a Smart Steward you should assess where you are. Is your nonprofit already at the edge of its flight envelope? Many nonprofits are already under-resourced, under-funded, under administered. As you'll see in the next chapter, most don't have the cash to expand either.

What you don't want to do is to pile more work (even though it will result in more mission) on an organization that is already overburdened. The proverbial straw that broke the camel's back is a cautionary tale you need to keep in mind.

Current capacity is hard to objectively measure, but not impossible. While the specific metrics will vary organization by organization, here are some things to look at.

Look at Your Management Staff Load   As I said above, most organizations are under-administered. I often tell audiences that their personal Full Time Equivalent (FTE) count has risen: Five years ago, they probably only had two FTE living in their bodies, now they may have three, four, or five. While sort of funny, it's also true. Just because funding goes down, it doesn't mean that management responsibilities do. To take a look at this, start by looking at your organizational chart from five years back and comparing it to now. Are there fewer managers per line staff person? Have some functions (like accounting or IT) had a reduction in staff while the organization has grown?

Slow and steady staff burdening often goes unnoticed until it is a crisis, like the frog in the slowly heating pot. You need to be looking out for this, starting now. There is of course, no clear-cut measure, but it will get you started. Some other tell-tale signs of staff being over capacity include the following.

Staff Satisfaction
I hope you're already measuring staff satisfaction regularly. This kind of surveying is crucial to making sure you don't miss what's going on at the level of service provision. Of course, comparative data over time is also key—are you doing better or worse than prior years? What about the comments? Do they show an issue you need to drill down into? This survey can be an early window into staff that are overworked.

Staff Turnover
Turnover is a tricky thing to use as a metric. Some turnover rates that seem high are really pretty good in context of national numbers, while too low a turnover can hold an organization's growth back. What you

want to look for is spikes over time, as well as spikes in certain programs or administrative areas.

Use of Sick Days
Sick days can go both ways. If people think they can't take the time to be sick, they'll come in sick—and get everyone else sick. On the other hand, if people are miserable at work since they feel overwhelmed, this number may rise steeply. Monitor this closely.

Use of Vacation Days
In most overburdened organizations, the management staff doesn't take much if any vacation. This is a bad thing—we all need a break. If this number is low and getting worse, you're near or at capacity.

Look at Your Quality Indicators I assume you have a quality-assurance program or monitoring system. Take a look at that on a regular basis (perhaps every six months) and compare the results over time. Are you having more problems? Is your accreditation or licensing review turning up more negative findings than in the past? Again, these are issues that need to concern you and get fixed before you consider growing any more.

Remember: Cash Equals Oxygen

We'll discuss cash (and quality) at length in the next chapter, but for now, remember that in a growth situation, you soak up amazing amounts of cash. Do you have adequate and available cash on hand now, before you grow? How much do you need? We'll see in Chapter 6.

What about HR, IT, and Other Administrative Functions?

So often in nonprofits, these are forgotten when growth is being considered. Sadly the example for such oversight comes from funders who only want to fund direct costs or are obsessed with admin percentages, which is a totally useless metric, but causes CEOs everywhere to pause before making needed additions to their back offices.

Nevertheless, you need to talk through capacity to grow with your managers in each of these areas. If the discussion of 5 or 10 percent growth next year causes them to nearly faint, drill down some more and see what's going on. They may well have been toughing it out at present work levels, trying not to add to your burden, but when faced with significant growth realize that they are at or over the breaking point.

When Do You Add Capacity?

This is a tough, tough issue. If you're like most managers, you will have added some capacity too soon and some too late during your career. For some budget items, like direct service staff, it's more straightforward; you have to have them in place before you can open your new service, right? True, but do you staff for your lowball expectations of demand, for your midline, or for the top end? In terms of space, how much more work can you cram into your current space before you expand? Your staff are griping that they're crawling all over each other, but if you rent (or purchase) new space, renovate it, and then your contracts are cancelled—what then?

If this hemming and hawing (also known as management deliberation) sounds familiar, join the club. The math is not simple arithmetic; there are a ton of unknowns. You have to factor in your organizational financial stability, you and your boards' risk-taking quotient, and your confidence that your contracts/grants/fundraising will continue at least at their current pace.

Lakeview Capacity   When Mark arrived, he knew he wanted to continue growing the church. He first needed to transition the governance of the organization from, as he puts it, "Board governed to elder guided," and transitioned staff from "*doing* ministry to *leading* ministries through volunteers." These two actions would free staff up to manage and lead the organization. To fuel growth, the church added a third worship service and introduced a contemporary worship style for two of its three services to encourage the growth of younger members and young families. Mark also hired significantly, including five "20-something team members who would introduce a fresh wave of ministry . . . ."

Mark did this (and lots, lots more) knowing that church giving had been steadily growing: Lakeview's congregation had always been (and continues to be) incredibly generous in their support of the church. So the finances were reasonably secure. But, he also knew he'd need to increase both staff and volunteers and have them up and running sooner rather than later if the church was to grow while also supporting other key initiatives, such as an improved guest experience, increased community outreach, and supporting more missions.

Mark had many balls in the air at once. He's a self-professed "instinctive" leader, a "next step guy, not a next three steps guy." That said, he's rounded out his administrative team with long-range thinkers as well, and people who can run the numbers on growth.

Any large growth strategy has a ton of moving parts. It helps, as in Lakeview's case, if the financial situation is solid to start with, but there are still many things that can go wrong, and that need to be evaluated This is why, for any large project, you need to do a business plan. Part of that plan is lining up the assumptions upon which you base your decision to go ahead. Another part of the plan is assessing both your capacity and capability, and yet a third part is your startup sequence, which will include how and when you ramp up your capacity in any areas needed.

 HANDS ON: For many, if not most, nonprofits, having the skill of business planning on their staff (or board) is a competence they can no longer do without. If you're not a large enough organization to have someone assigned to this task, consider adding it to your board or volunteer skillset as you recruit new volunteers. ∎

A Capacity Checklist before Growing

I make no apologies: I'm a list guy. I make a to-do list for each day and week, have running lists of work and home projects, my wife and I have an on-going list of groceries and other supplies needed when we run errands. It works for us, keeps us from forgetting things (increasingly important when you get to be our age!), and reduces down time—I never have to wonder about "What's next?," I just look at the list.

For large events such as a new contract or expansion in your organization, a checklist is essential. You'll have people to call, licenses to obtain, contracts to review, people to hire. What can easily get lost is the checking on capacity. So, I've started (note, only *started*) your list for you. Expand and add to this as needed, but use the list to help you decide whether you can grow, how much it will cost you to grow, and make sure all the problems are resolved *before* you actually start out on your growth path.

☐ Do we have adequate space to provide quality services?
☐ Do we have the capacity to continue quality service provision at our current services? (more on this in the next chapter)
☐ Is our IT capable of handling the growth with its current infrastructure, equipment, software, and security?
☐ Is our HR adequately staffed to support staff growth?
☐ Is there any capacity backfill we need to do (that we may have neglected or put off earlier) that needs to be completed before we start?
☐ Do any of our policies and procedures need review or update to accommodate our new growth?
☐ How much staff growth will be required and are the needed skills available?
☐ Do we have enough cash to afford the growth we are planning? (more on this in the next chapter)

In looking at this list, I'm sure you see a lot of work, but it's essential to do this part of the work *before* you grow, so that you can stage your capacity building to match up with service needs, cash availability, and management-oversight capacity. It's Smart Stewardship at its best.

You have to have both the capacity and the capability to grow, but it's also true that examining your capability and capacity—even if you don't plan a major new initiative—allows you to focus on what you do well and look down the road to see what you need to do well going forward. Such a review also lets you take a hard look at your current capacity, which may show that your staff and volunteers are already at the breaking point.

Too many of us in the nonprofit sector always start with "Yes!" when offered a chance to help. In fact, few, if any of us, came to the sector to say no. That's fundamentally a good thing. The problem comes when we say Yes, Yes, Yes! over and over without making sure that we really can do what we're promising. Think of my story about my takeoff adventure. I had said yes too quickly, and it could have turned out much worse than just one very relieved pilot.

You don't want to crash your organization for any reason. You're in the mission for the long haul and people depend on you to be there this year, next, and far into the future. Figuring out what you're best at (and doing more of that), confessing where you don't excel (and getting help or getting out), and constantly evaluating your capacity to do the things you've promised the community all figure in to your ability to do great mission for many years to come.

Recap

In this chapter, you learned how to evaluate both your capabilities and your capacity to grow. We started by looking at core competencies. I gave you two key takeaways which were:

- The people you serve deserve to be served better than just adequately.
- If you're considering expanding as a policy, find out what you're really good at—and do more of that.

Finding out what you're really good at is called a core competence. I showed you the classic three-part definition of a core competence, which was:

1. It provides consumer benefits;
2. It is not easy for competitors to imitate;
3. It can be leveraged widely to many products and markets.

But, since this is defined for the for-profit world, I provided you with my nonprofit, three-part set of core-competence criteria:

1. Do we have objective evidence (accreditation or outcome measures, for example) that our skill in this area is exceptional?
2. Can this core skill be used/transferred across our organization?
3. Do we have highly educated and experienced people leading in this area of our organization?
4. Does this competence make us more mission capable?

I provided you with a sequence of how to discover your own core competencies, urged you to do it with wide collaboration, and gave you a tool to use in the process.

Next we turned to looking down the road a bit and predicting what core competencies you may need five years from now, and discussed ways to get a jump on that need.

After that, we looked at your current capacity, starting with a review of a variety of capacities including people, space, money, and time, as well as specific skills such as Human Resources and Technology. I showed you both why it's key to know when you're close to overflowing in these areas and how to measure from internal data you probably already have.

Finally, we went through a starting checklist for you to use if you're thinking about growing quickly or into a new area of service, a new population, or a new part of your community.

Now that we've seen how to evaluate both your capabilities and your capacity, it's time to look at the costs of growth. There are things organizations run out of in rapid growth situations: cash and quality. Your nonprofit can't afford to be lacking in either. In the next chapter, I'll show you how to measure the cash cost, show you how and why your service quality levels are at risk, and give you some tools to avoid a quality crash.

Discussion Questions

1. Let's start with capability, or as Peter reminds us, core competence. What are we really good at? Let's use the tool he provides us, fill it in for our services, and see what we come up with.
2. Okay, now that we know what we're really good at, we also know the areas where we don't stand out. What should we do about these? Do we ramp up our skill set, get out of that business, or delegate or contract out the work?

(*continued*)

3. Looking five years down the road, we know from our strategic plan and marketing data where things are heading. What new skills do we need to acquire and get really good at? Peter listed things like focused development and technology (particularly social networks). Do those apply to us? Are there others?
4. What resources do we have (or can we find) to help us improve our skills? How can we get this into the budget on an ongoing basis?
5. Let's pick an example of a new service or expansion that we went through and look at when we added capacity. Did we do it too soon, too late, or just right? How can we learn from that experience?

CHAPTER 6

Understanding the True Cost of Growth

Chapter Thumbnail

Overview
What Growth Does to An Organization
How to Run Out Of Cash
How to Run Out of Quality
Is a No-Growth or Slow-Growth Policy Smart Stewardship?
Recap

Overview

Nearly all nonprofits want to grow their mission capability. They want to do more mission, help more people, and affect more positive change. Mission is why you and your staff show up each day, so why wouldn't you want to do more? Your board may also be focused on growth, as many of them are from the business world, where the concept of regular growth is not only worshiped but rarely, if ever, challenged.

I've said this earlier in the book: I have no problem with organizations growing, whether they be for-profit or nonprofit. I understand the mission urge, the peer pressure, the board and funder pressure (more on that in a minute), and the community pressure to do more good and help those in need. I get that.

But I also cannot responsibly let the issue of growth go unaddressed without making sure that you fully understand the cost of growth. I've seen both excellent and not-so-great nonprofits torn apart by rapid growth scenarios. We've already talked (in Chapter 5) about competence and capacity and both are strained by growth. We've discussed a focus on mission and values, and these, too, are stressed in growth situations (Chapter 4), if by no more than the all-too-common act in many nonprofits of chasing the money.

In this chapter, I want you to take the time to read through and understand at the ground level what the costs are of growing, not to turn you away from growth, but rather to make sure you anticipate the two most common downfalls of growth, which are running out of cash and running out of quality. I don't want you to run out of either.

In this chapter, we'll start by looking at what growth does (both good and bad) for a nonprofit. I'll rant a bit about funders who demand that you always "take the idea to scale" and then give you some examples of how our case study organizations (Goodwill Industries of North Georgia [GING], Peckham, and Lakeview Community Church) managed to avoid falling into the cash and quality traps while growing in organizations.

Next, I'll show you how to run out of cash—so that you can avoid doing just that in your organization. We'll look at an example of how much cash you use up in a simple, common grant situation, and I'll give you a tool to let you calculate your own cash load as you grow.

Then, we'll turn to quality, and I'll show you a second time how to run out of something that you can't afford to be without. We'll talk through quality from a number of angles and help you make sure you don't lose the high levels of quality you've worked so hard to attain.

We'll close the chapter by considering a no or slow-growth policy. I'll show you why some organizations have done just that, and how it turned out for them.

By the end of the chapter, you'll understand better where the soft spots are in the grow, grow, grow mantra, and how to avoid them. You'll know how to figure out your cash costs, avoid quality reductions, and, in short, make sure that your well-intentioned and laudable plans to grow more mission don't wind you up on the dark side of The Force.

What Growth Does to an Organization

What's the definition of a nonprofit steward? There are many, but mine is:

> *"A nonprofit steward is someone who consistently leads the organization in managing the resources of the community in a manner that maximizes its mission effectiveness."*

That definition was the foundation of my 2004 book *Nonprofit Stewardship; A Better Way to Lead Your Mission-Based Organization*. It's still true, I still support the definition, but for our purposes here I want to focus on the idea of "maximizing mission effectiveness."

What it doesn't say is maximizing mission. It doesn't require you, as a steward to do more mission, just better and more effective mission. And for many nonprofits, growth—particularly rapid growth—can hurt the organization in two places first: cash and quality. Since money enables mission, cash is crucial. Since quality is at risk, growth may cause us to violate the part of the stewardship definition that notes the need for "high quality mission."

You've all heard or read about personal stress; that too much stress can be harmful to your health, and even result in disease and/or death. Moreover the stress does not have to be "bad." Inside your body, "good" stress such as planning a wedding, starting a new job, or the birth of a child has almost the same negative affect as bad stress such as losing a job or a romantic breakup.

And stress shows up in different, often strange ways. Weight loss (or gain) lack of sleep (or sleeping too much), a rash, a tic, loss of focus on immediate tasks, odd aches and pains, all of these and many more can be the result of stress on your body. In short, stress is stress, and its affects show up in unexpected places.

It's the same in our organization. Growth, doing more mission, helping more people is good stress on the organization. But it's still stress, and it can result in unpredictable changes in your organization, unless you plan, and stay vigilant and flexible.

GING Growth

GING has grown nearly five-fold (from just a bit more than $20 million in revenue to north of $100 million) in the decade ending in 2011. One of the keys to this kind of growth is great middle management, and GING invests heavily in its managers, with constant training, guidance, and inclusion in the growth strategies of the organization. As noted earlier, a mid-management team (not the executive staff) revised the GING mission. This kind of mid-manager impact is not unusual, and it results in higher morale and less turnover. The GING executive staff sees this low turnover as crucial to high-quality growth.

Peckham Growth

Peckham had intentionally stayed within the geographic area around Lansing, Michigan, since its focus on culture first was (and is) so strong. A few years ago, it was asked by a federal contractor to work a contract in Iowa, its first venture out of state. This work, while eventually successful, "took much, much, *much* more time and effort than any of us envisioned," Mitch Tomlinson, the chief executive officer (CEO), noted. "We had all kinds of unforeseen challenges, but learned a great deal. We're now putting that learning to use in another out-of-state expansion."

Lakeview Growth

As noted earlier, Lakeview started in a good situation in terms of congregational generosity, but when Mark arrived, it was under-staffed in relation to its membership size. Mark could have staffed up even more than he did, but he emphasized that paid staff should lead ministry through volunteers. This strategy held down staff expenses while engaging more members in the ministry of the church. The challenge, of course, was to make that volunteer experience meaningful, and this required training of paid staff in volunteer leadership.

All three of these organizations worked their way through significant growth by paying attention to the key concerns of staff: quality and values. They grew at a reasonably fast rate, but managed (word used intentionally) their growth, they just didn't go for revenue increases and see what happened. It should also be noted that all three organizations started with financial stability already in place.

And, there still were stresses. The **GING** management team had to keep avoiding the temptation to stray from its core business as offers piled in. **Peckham** expanded into higher-tech contracting, which meant a very high (and expensive) learning curve. **Lakeview** also had hard choices: Grow at its current site with more services or build more. It decided to focus on spending more money on mission outreach as opposed to bricks and mortar.

But none of these decisions were quick, simple, or without detractors. They were the result of lengthy debates and discussion, and the outcome of lots of outreach for input from a variety of perspective in each organization.

How to Run Out of Cash

Almost all nonprofits have too little cash on hand at any given time. Sometimes this is the result of funder policies not letting the nonprofit keep what they earn (or tut-tutting when a nonprofit has two dimes to rub together), sometimes a result of poor long-term management on the part of the nonprofit, sometimes caused by a short-term crisis, or a combination of the above. And, if you don't have any cash cushion, as CEO, you lose a lot of sleep. I know a CEO who has been in her position for 20 years and who has fretted about making payroll twice a month for every one of those 20 years. When I asked her a few years back about why she hasn't built up any reserves, she looked like I had hit her: "We can't do that. People are in need. It's immoral for us to carry any money from one fiscal year to the next." So, her organization is *intentionally* cash poor.

While I understand her sentiment and admire her empathy for the people her organization serves, this is not Smart Stewardship. The quality of the space where the organization provides services is appalling, her staff turnover is high, there's no web site (thus impacting her fundraising efforts), and the next-longest-serving employee has only been there three years. And any delay in payments from key funders, or reductions in donations, and the doors close.

Not every nonprofit falls into the trap of being cash poor, but if you feel your organization is chronically cash short, you cannot, let me repeat, *cannot* grow. Growth sucks up cash like a giant vacuum cleaner. You need cash, and more importantly, *cash that you can spare*, to grow.

Here's the key takeaway for this issue. Cash equals oxygen. Cash buys you time to think, is insurance against funding cutbacks, and lets you sleep at night assured you can make rent at the beginning of the month. Cash lets you manage rather than just survive.

And growth? Growth is funded by cash. Remember my mantra earlier in the book: Money enables mission, but profits enable growth. Without profits (and profits that are retained, not immediately spent), you can't grow.

 FOR EXAMPLE: Let's do the numbers using a not-all-that-unusual example. A funder, who loves your services and has been a strong supporter, calls you and says, "We have a one year grant opportunity for you. We want you to expand Service X for the next year and measure the impact."

You are intrigued and excited: More mission! And, Service X is your core competence and serves your highest priority demographic. More high priority, high quality mission! The funder continues:

"You need to shoot me a financial projection, but we know you and trust your management. Also, send me a number of units of service based on a one year, $1 million grant. We'll go from there."

You are nearly speechless. $1 million? *One million dollars?* And full reimbursement? There's no risk! Then, you think, where's the catch? The funder continues,

"No worries about match. We want to get this project going, so we'll reimburse your costs fully. We'll reimburse you each month within 45 days of your billing us. Get back to me by the end of work tomorrow and we can make this month's contracting and approval cycle. Have a nice day."

Now there's an understatement, you think . . . a nice day . . . this is the best. Day. Ever. You shoot out of your chair to go share the news that your mission growth just went off the charts.

(continued)

(*continued*)

How does all this sound to you? Awesome? Unlikely? Yes on both counts of course. But while you have visions of mission growth dancing in your head, let's look at this amazing, high priority, no-risk mission opportunity in a bit more depth.

Let's assume you start the service at the beginning of the next month, which we'll call June 1. Let's also assume you can just start doing more mission from a standing start—no upfront expenses like more space, licensing, training, and so on. You and I both know we always have those expenses, but for now, just keep them in the back of your mind to add in later.

So, June 1 you start doing a *lot* more mission. On June 30, if you're like most nonprofits, you bill the funder, and the 45-day reimbursement clock starts. If the funder actually gets you the reimbursement in 45 days, that means you get paid on August 15, or 75 days after you started the expanded mission.

During those 75 days, what has your organization done? *Lots* of great, high priority mission. You've helped *lots* of people.

And spent *lots* of cash. *Lots.* How much? Let's do the math.

Take $1,000,000. Divide it by 365 to get a cash cost per day. The result is a daily cost of $2,739.73. Then, multiply the daily cost by the 75 days you have to wait for reimbursement. $2,739.73 times 75 equals **$205,479.45.**

That's a lowball calculation of the amount of money that goes out before you get paid. Ouch. And that's real cash going out the door, money that can't be used to pay rent or insurance or other staff payroll. Remember that the $205,000 does NOT include the startup costs we pushed aside earlier. So in nearly all cases the number would be higher, perhaps much higher, than $205,000. ■

Moral? To afford this no-risk, high-priority mission opportunity you need more than 20 percent of the grant total in hand, in cash, before you start. This money is called *working capital,* and it's the money you need between the time you make a product or provide a service and get paid. The more you grow, the more working capital you need, even if it's not in big, one-time $1,000,000 increments. The longer the funder takes to pay you, the more working capital you need. The higher your startup costs are, the more working capital you need.

Where does this working capital come from? From prior years' earnings. If you haven't put funds aside, you can't take advantage of opportunities as they arise. And, by the way, no bank is going to lend you funds to cover this grant's working capital. Loans are paid back by profits, and this grant, while fully reimbursing your costs, does not include a profit. And you can't sell stock in your nonprofit—that's only for for-profit firms. So, you need to be making a profit to grow.

Remember my mantra from earlier in the book: Money enables mission, but profit enables more mission. And here we are with a perfect example. Your nonprofit's prior profits allow you to take the $1,000,000. If you haven't made the profit and set it aside, all you're doing is running out of cash.

 HANDS ON: This is why so many nonprofits who have a budget goal of breaking even and, like my CEO friend, feel that making a profit is wrong, are always out of cash as they grow, even if that growth is minimal. They make the mistake of thinking that if their income and expense report shows a break even that they should have enough cash to pay the bills. Fatal error. Accrual and cash are different, and a break-even profit and loss (P&L) does not mean that your cash in and cash out match for the fiscal year. ∎

Again, my point here is that growth, any growth, sucks up cash. Your organization has working capital invested in your operations now. Even if you grow organically, you'll need more. Conversely, if programs end, it frees up working capital for you.

Predicting the Cash Cost of Growth

Predicting working capital costs can be complex, particularly if your income comes from a wide variety of sources. This is why you do a business plan for big, new programs, but what about organic, year to year growth? I have two tools for you to use.

Cash-Flow Projection   Every nonprofit, including yours, should have a cash-flow projection report that shows cash in, out, and a balance six months into the future. This projection is a key management tool, as well as a key fiduciary report for your board. Income and expense statements are important, balance sheets are nice, but cash equals oxygen. Without it, your organization dies. Have this projection on a spreadsheet and update it regularly.

Remember, this is cash, so the report shows what are termed receipts and disbursements, not income and expense, which are for your accrual-based P&L. Receipts are cash in the door in checks received or electronic transfers to your checking accounts. Disbursements are the same—cash out or checks or payments sent. And remember, cash almost always comes in later than we expect and goes out at payroll and payroll tax time.

For the next month, and the following five months, your projection should show starting cash, receipts, disbursements, and ending cash. The projection will be the most accurate in the first month, of course, and less

EXHIBIT 6-1 Sample Cash Need Projection Spreadsheet

Programs	Startup Costs	Current Budget	Next Year Budget	Days Payable This Year	Days Payable Next Year	CASH NEED
Residential	0	440,000	480,000	95	95	**10,959**
Day	0	327,500	410,000	56	56	**12,658**
Outreach	0	457,000	395,000	55	55	**−9,342**
Hot lunch	0	110,000	115,000	45	45	**616**
Prevention (new)	45,000	0	197,000	0	65	**80,082**
					Total Cash Need	**94,973**

to-the-penny accurate as you go forward in time, but you're looking for trends here, not to-the-cent accuracy.

An Organic Growth Tool

While some nonprofits have rapid growth, many of us opt for the regular, steady, organic growth model. But here, too, working capital is needed. Exhibit 6.1 is an example of a spreadsheet that was done at the time of budgeting for a human services nonprofit. You'll see its four programs, the days payable which often change, and that's noted. Remember, if the budget goes up (residential is an example of this in Exhibit 6.1), your working capital needs increase. If the budget stays the same, but the days payable increase, you'll need more cash. If budget decreases, cash is freed up.

This example shows four areas of operation, residential, day, outreach, and hot lunch. As can be seen from the example, only outreach is shrinking next year. A new program, prevention is starting up. For this agency, the growth of three programs, the addition of one, and the reduction of another results in a $94,973 increase in working capital obligations. This means that the organization has to find $95,000 in un-obligated cash during the year, some before it starts the year, some during the year. If it can't, the nonprofit can't afford the growth it is budgeting for.

One last prompt: here's the way the calculation for the cash need in the DAY program was done.

Step 1	**410,000 − 327,500 = 82,500 in new cash needs**
Step 2	**82,500 ÷ 365 = 226.03 per day in new cash needs**
Step 3	**226.03 × 56 days = 12,658 in cash needs for the program**

One last time: *cash equals oxygen,* and growth soaks up cash. Be prepared, and for most nonprofits that means start putting aside cash now to fund mission growth down the road.

But what about the other growth cost that I talked about, the cost of quality? Let's take a look at this all important component of Smart Stewardship.

How to Run Out of Quality

Quality, Quality, Quality. It's a mantra that Smart Stewards repeat over and over, particularly after we've figured out what our core competencies are. We want the people that we serve to be served well. The word *quality, best practices* or *world class* often shows up in our mission and values statements. We seek accreditation to assure that we are, in fact, doing best practices, and often have quality assurance policies, particularly if our organization has a variety of sites, or very time- and expertise-intensive services.

All of which is to say that quality assurance is on our minds so much, and so often such a large part of the daily and weekly norm, that it's easy to lose focus on it even though it's a priority.

 FOR EXAMPLE: In the last chapter, I told you a somewhat lengthy story about a piloting experience that pushed my plane's flight envelope. Rest assured, this example is much shorter! In navigation, it would seem obvious that direction of flight is important. If you need to fly a course due west ("two-seven-zero" to a pilot) you have to both set the course and make mid-course corrections to achieve it. There are cross winds to contend with on most flights, they can vary greatly, and easily affect your aircraft's direction of flight.

You're also assigned a specific altitude by Air Traffic Control, and you must stay at that altitude. Straying from your assigned altitude can be very dangerous, as other aircraft may be assigned to go in an opposite direction only 500 or 1,000 feet above or below your assigned altitude. Aircraft can easily deviate from their assigned altitude slowly but surely due to decreased weight (from fuel use) and other factors.

Think of a course and altitude setting as your quality setting. It's important, even crucial. You do it without thinking, since it becomes natural muscle memory after a bit of experience. But it's easy to get distracted, to go off course, both in the air and in your organization. You have to pay constant attention, even if you have an auto-pilot.

I noted in the first chapter that there's a rule in flying: "Stop paying attention for three seconds and you're off course or off altitude." My experience is that this is true, in the air and on the ground in organizations. ■

We have to stay focused on the details of quality, make it a cultural norm, and share the responsibility for quality at both the staff and board levels.

And here's where growth or contraction, particularly if it's rapid, can result in deteriorating quality—it's distracting to everyone. Sometimes that distraction is a function of time, sometimes it's a function of location.

 FOR EXAMPLE: Your organization is offered the opportunity to provide services in an adjacent town or county, a two-hour drive from your main location. The service in question is one you already do very well. This is your first experience with a remote facility startup, and you study the best practices and other organizations' experiences carefully before going ahead. You have the cash, quality, and competence in the person of your service manager, who we'll name Susan. Susan has been with you for 15 years and is a fabulous manager. She and her staff provide truly excellent services, which is why you received the offer to expand.

If you're like most managers, who do you send to the town two hours down the road to start and supervise the expansion? Someone with little experience? Someone from the local community who you don't know? No, if you're like most managers, you send Susan, the best you've got.

Which is great for the people in the new location (and, we hope, for Susan). But the question is this: What happens to the level of quality at your main location once Susan is no longer there eight to ten hours a day. Whether she moves to the new town or commutes, she can't be on site at the home office as much as before. If you're already under-administered, there's a real risk of a quality fall-off here, one that needs to be attended to. ▪

So, just as with competence, capacity, and cash, we need to consider the quality impact of our growth, and do that on two levels. We need to assure that our *current* services remain at their current levels of quality (or improve) during growth, and we need to assure that any *new* services are also provided at a high level of quality from day one.

 HANDS ON: Core competence certainly helps here, but you have to put in an extra dose of quality-assurance effort from everyone and be up front with the fact that the stress of growth or contraction can result in a reduction in quality. Talk to your staff and have them talk to their direct reports coaching, urging, and cajoling people into continuing to pay attention to the levels of quality and being on the lookout for ways that management can help line staff to make sure there are no quality lapses. Be ready to help and remember, like so many other values, quality needs to be led visibly from the front. ▪

Is a No-Growth or Slow-Growth Policy Smart Stewardship?

This chapter has focused on exposing you to the true costs and risks that growth, particularly rapid growth, poses to your mission. That said, you're probably thinking, "Okay, got it, we'll grow and do our best to minimize the downsides of doing more mission."

And that's fine. I certainly understand the visceral desire most of us have to do more mission, do more good. Our conscience pushes us that way, as do our board and funders (more on that in a little bit). Additionally, as I said at the beginning of the chapter, our entire society is focused on more, more, more, grow, grow, grow. Thus the cultural norm tells us that growth is good and we don't give it much of a second thought.

But what if we traded a policy of growth for a policy of the highest quality possible? While that trade off is not necessarily quid pro quo (that less growth will mean higher quality or that rapid growth means poor quality) it does bring into focus the fact that you only have so much time and money to use for mission, and that growing does channel some of your resources away from a focus on the here and now.

Bo Burlingham has written a terrific book on this phenomena in the for-profit world. It's called *Small Giants; Companies That Choose to Be Great Rather than Big,* and I highly recommend it as a read for you before you do your next strategic planning session. It will force you to think a bit differently about growth. Here's some text from the book cover:

> *"It's a widely accepted axiom of business that great companies grow their revenues and profits year after year. Yet quietly, under the radar, some entrepreneurs have rejected the pressure of endless growth to focus on more satisfying business goals. Goals like being great at what they do . . . creating a great place to work . . . providing great customer service . . . making great contributions to their communities . . . and finding great ways to lead their lives."*

I've talked with many a successful nonprofit CEO who is wistful about the days when the organization was smaller. "I *hate* having to have everyone wear a name tag," says one friend. She recounts that one of her personal goals was always to be able to know all her employees and volunteers by name:

> *"That slipped away as our reputation grew, funders came to us with more service opportunities, and we went from having 50 employees to 1,500 in six or seven years. I love how much mission we do, but sometimes worry that we've lost our sense of self, our ability to get and keep everyone on the same page."*

So is small better? For some organizations, certainly. And, staying small (or not growing) is not a bad choice for most nonprofits in certain situations. For example, a great number of nonprofits (and for-profits) put off growth decisions in the teeth of the 2008 to 2009 Great Recession, preferring (wisely, I think) to wait a bit before taking on obligations that they might not be able to keep.

My suggestion here is to regularly revisit your ability as well as your organizational desire to grow. That's why you have strategic plans and discussions, why you need to take the time to step back from the week-to-week work and do some larger scale thinking. What if you could be the best mission provider and the best place to work, and focused on the unique needs of your community and be a great place to volunteer, and provide fabulous customer service to all your customers? While staying your current size doesn't guarantee any of these characteristics appearing spontaneously, focusing all your time, money, and energy on internal improvements (even if only for a few years) could well result in at least some of those lofty goals being achieved.

All I'm asking you to do as a Smart Steward is to ask the questions, and not automatically go with the "growth is always good" flow.

On Going to Scale

Just a bit earlier in this chapter I referred to the pressure/encouragement that boards and funders put on nonprofits to grow their mission output. I need to take a minute right here to talk about that in more detail, at least regarding the current state of funder's pushing nonprofits to grow, sometimes at a grievous cost. NOTE: Chapter 8 is all about Going to Scale, but I feel it's important here to make the points I'm about to, since they relate closely to the cost of growth.

As this book is published, we're in our third or fourth year of a growing trend, particularly in foundations of funders focusing on ideas that can be "replicated and taken to scale." On the surface, and from the funders' point of view, this makes eminent sense: If I fund one project in one city and it can be replicated elsewhere, I get more bang for the buck. The problem with this, as with so many ideas generated at the 30,000-foot level, comes on the ground. Nonprofits seeking funding are forced (implicitly or explicitly) to favor ideas that can work broadly. This causes them to turn away from going after more customized solutions to local (and often unique) problems that can help their own community, and focus instead on replicable, often less customized ideas that can be scaled and meet the funders' wants.

Moreover, in seeking models that can be duplicated elsewhere, the 30,000-foot view forgets that no model is replicable without exactly the right people. What causes a program or solution to work in one place is a potpourri of the location, the issue, the people, the timing, the politics, even the geography. To assume you can just replicate the model elsewhere is . . . naive, and not borne out by experience. It takes a ton of work (and money) and adjustment to the local situation on the ground.

Further, by accepting funding that urges them to go to scale with their idea, nonprofits (and the funders) often forget the truth on the ground that this chapter focuses on: In rapid-growth situations, the two things that an organization most easily runs out of are quality and cash. If growth is the priority, what do you do, take your worst manager to open your new expanded facility or location? No, as we noted previously, you take your best person—and in doing so remove that best person from what he or she is doing now—awesome, high-quality mission.

And, in many organizations that have been beaten down by funders' focus on low administrative costs, there aren't more managers to just plug into the program that your best manager just left. So the funder may well have first left the nonprofit under-administered but now wants it to grow.

Speaking of under-administered, let's get to the underfunding in terms of the cash cost of growth. This is huge, and, again, mostly underappreciated by funders. The funding options I often see in the nonprofit world are for a *one-time* grant, with the desired outcome of a scalable, replicable idea. If the idea fails, no more funding.

What happens in the for-profit, venture capital (VC) world? A great idea gets an initial round of funding with several more rounds of financing as the business grows. Why? Because, as you already know, growth sucks up cash like a giant vacuum cleaner. And, venture capitalists know that even the best idea will morph and change over time as implementation experience is added to the mix. There's no model, just an idea trying to survive and thrive in the current situation on the ground. Therefore, multiple funding rounds are expected and they allow the cash needed to be re-evaluated as time passes and experience grows. Nonprofit funders could learn a lot from embedding themselves in a VC firm for a year.

The bottom line for me is to be very, very careful when someone tells you to go to scale. Look at all the costs of taking the money: The stress on your current program, the potential loss of focus, the cash cost of growth, and look at it all before you obligate your organization. One other help for you: Chapter 8 is dedicated to the issue of Going to Scale. Check there before you set off on a journey you can't finish.

One last time, growth of mission is good. That said, growth of mission is not necessarily good for every nonprofit, and certainly not for every nonprofit in every situation. Only you, your senior management, and your board can decide what your situation is, but if you don't consider competence, capacity, cash, and quality before you start down the growth road, you may wind up hurting rather than helping the people you are in business to serve.

So, my strong suggestion is to posit these questions to your group: Are we ready to grow? If not, what do we need to do to get ready? Given our current situation does a focus on quality rather than growth make more sense?

I'm not suggesting that a slow-growth or no-growth (for a while) policy is best for your nonprofit, but it is one choice, and one that many organizations (for profit and nonprofit) are taking.

Recap

In this chapter, we examined the cost of growth for your nonprofit. While always supporting the concept of growth to do more mission, I've seen far too many organizations crash and burn while seeking to do more good. Thus, the information in this chapter.

We started by discussing the cost of growth, and looked at examples from GING, Lakeview, and Peckham. You heard me talk about the fact that growth is a good kind of stress, but stress nonetheless. Stress shows up in weird ways and unexpected places, and you have to be watching for it all the time.

There are two places in your nonprofit that will show predictable stress marks from growth: Cash flow and quality of service, and the next two sections covered those in detail. I showed you a common example of what's termed working capital needs for a grant, and then a way to calculate your own cash needs in a growth scenario so that you can stay ahead of the cash curve. Remember: *Cash equals oxygen*.

Next, we looked at quality and all the ways that it can slide if you're growing (or shrinking). You lose your focus on quality and you'll lose funding, your best staff, and your ability to look at yourself in the mirror. I gave you some ways to avoid this fate, most importantly paying constant attention to the details and leading the quality value visibly, and from the front.

Finally, we talked through a consideration of a no-growth or slow growth policy. I provided you some references on this method of running your nonprofit and, while I know it's not for every CEO or every organization, it does have its benefits.

I hope in this chapter, and the last one on capacity and capability, you realized that you can damage your nonprofit (perhaps fatally) by setting out on a growth path before you're ready. If you don't have all four of these: the cash, the capacity, the quality assurance mechanisms, and the core competencies, you are putting your nonprofit, your mission, and the services you provide to the people who depend on you at risk. I trust you'll look before you leap. All Smart Stewards do.

With that due diligence behind us, let's turn to the fun stuff—new ideas, innovation, staying cutting edge. Nearly all of us want this in our organizations, but how can we develop an innovation culture, one that breeds new ideas all the time? That's the subject of our next chapter.

Discussion Questions

1. Have any of us been in situations where starting a new program or new location have put undue stress on the organization? Let's tell the stories and see what we can learn.
2. What about cash? Do our funders have a problem with us retaining cash? What about our board? Our staff?
3. How can we be better about assuring that our quality levels stay high throughout either an expansion or a contraction of services? What are the most important two or three things we can do?
4. Have we just assumed that growth is good? What about the idea of staying at our current size and simply being the best at what we do? How does that affect our mission commitment?
5. Which of these issues should we bring to our next strategic planning retreat or strategic discussion session for our board?

CHAPTER 7

Making Innovation the Norm

Chapter Thumbnail

Overview

Up to now in this book, we've talked about mission, values, the Smart Stewardship decision tree, and some key points on that tree, including capacity, capabilities, cash, and quality. All those are important, and I'm sure that at times I've seemed more like a scold than an inspirational coach, shaking my finger at you reminding you to check your cash flow, remember quality, stay on mission.

In this chapter, we have a change of scenery. We're going to discuss ways for you to be constantly getting better. Smart Stewards embrace other's best practices, at least when those practices sync up with their nonprofit's mission and values. But Smart Stewards also *add* to best practices by innovating all the time.

Making innovation *a* norm in your nonprofit should be an organizational goal. Making innovation *the* norm should be a cultural quest. Pursuing regular and constant innovation at every level, by every staff member and volunteer, by all your Smart Stewards, is key to being the best mission-based organization possible.

In this chapter we'll talk about how to do just that in ways you might not previously have thought made sense. We'll start by looking at why innovation seems (and in some cases is) so hard. I'll show you that innovation goes on around us every day, and that we're more innovative than we give our-selves credit for. Then we'll turn to the big secret: Innovation is easier if we do it collaboratively.

None of us can come up with the big idea, the big jump forward every day or even every week. The truth is that we have access to all kinds of good ideas if we just give up the burden of having to personally be the savior of our organization. If we practice what I call collaborative innovation, we can get better on all fronts a whole lot faster. I'll show you what I mean by col-laborative innovating and how your nonprofit can practice it. It's one of the linchpins of Smart Stewardship and, if you're willing to share the burden, a huge boon to your mission capability and quality of services.

I'll next show you some innovation tools and resources you can use, and finally, we'll cover how to do what I call "baking constant innovation" into your organization, making it not exceptional, but the norm. Understand, if you can make innovation the norm, you turn your organization into an exceptional one, one that *defines* best practice to others. How cool is that?

Let's get going.

Why Does Innovation Seem So Hard?

I've done perhaps two dozen presentations and workshops on innovation over the past few years and when you get the chance to really talk to people about their innovation efforts I'm told over and over "I'm no Einstein," or "I just never seem to come up with the big idea," or "Innovation—that's for techies and scientists, not me." Worse is when I hear chief executive officers (CEOs) saying words to the effect that they feel enormous pressure to inno-vate because it's *their* job (and no one else's) to solve problems. And these responses accurately sum up the biggest two barriers when we talk about becoming an innovative organization.

First is the assumption that *innovation* only means big ideas, big changes, big improvements. So, since I can't regularly come up with the big idea or big change, I'm not a good innovator. Pair this with the second mis-conception that, as CEO (or senior management), it's your job to solve all problems and come up with all improvements (which is far, far more preva-lent than you would think) and you have a recipe for innovation aversion. Let's deal with these issues in order.

I understand why someone would be put off if they believed that, in order to have the moniker of innovative on their resume, they have to have cured cancer. Imagine how few people would begin a jogging regimen if they believed they had to run a marathon a week later. The good news here is that the idea that innovation is only the invention of the light bulb, of crop rotation, or the theory of relativity is wrong. Flat wrong.

Innovation happens all around us every day, and, believe it or not, we innovate constantly, usually in small ways. We figure out a better commute to work, how to load the dishwasher more efficiently, a new way to get through to our teenagers, a new playlist for our mp3 player. Think for a minute about the things you do just a bit differently than you did a few weeks back. You probably don't even notice them, but they are there. You do your hair differently, changed the desktop image on your computer, figured out a new app for your smart phone.

If you still don't believe me, think about parents, a huge subset of the population. All through parenting, we innovate because we have to change the way we act, interact, react, protect, advocate, let go, supervise, reward, punish, and guide our children. Why? Because although parenting is the most important thing we ever do, there's no manual for it, and the children are always changing, growing, meeting new friends, going to a new school, learning how to ride a bike, and so on. So we have to accommodate the new situation and try to be the best possible parents we can for the sake of our kids. We make small adaptations every day, every week. That's one kind of constant innovation, and if you're a parent or grandparent, you know exactly what I mean.

Look at the bell curve in Exhibit 7.1. On the left end, you see the small innovations we've discussed, and on the other end the big, eureka innovations like the theory of relativity.

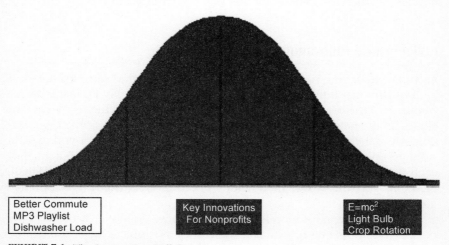

Better Commute	Key Innovations	$E=mc^2$
MP3 Playlist	For Nonprofits	Light Bulb
Dishwasher Load		Crop Rotation

EXHIBIT 7.1 The Innovation Bell Curve

The innovations on the tails (the ends) of the curve don't have much impact on the day to day activities of our nonprofit. What you want to focus on is the innovations in the center, the ones labeled "Key Innovations for Nonprofits." These kinds of innovations are the ones that make your non-profit more mission effective, that improve staff morale, that increase your amount, quality, effectiveness, and efficiency of mission production. If your values include the terms best practice, world class, or cutting edge, innovat-ing is a must.

Again, here, you've already done innovation in your organization and are probably doing it this week in some fashion. Every improvement in re-cord-keeping or office organization, every tweak in service delivery, every improvement to your web site or FaceBook page, every new form of com-munity outreach or application of what another organization is doing is in-novation. You're already there. The question is twofold: Are you essentially coming up with all these improvements on your own or with just a few man-agers, and how can you get more innovation going on a larger scale?

That brings us to our second barrier, the one I call "I'm the boss, so I solve the problems." This is common, and misguided. None of us, let me repeat that, *none* of us can solve all of our organization's problems, or can even come up with the best solutions to the ones we do solve. We only have one brain, one perspective, one set of training, and 24 hours in the day. If we believe that we, and we alone bear the innovation/problem solving bur-den we a) are not Smart Stewards, and b) are holding our nonprofit back.

John Chambers, the CEO of Cisco, has a wonderful line about this situa-tion. "No one of us is as smart as all of us." I completely agree, and the good news is that there's a solution for this, and it's our next topic.

Collaborative Innovation

As a steward of your nonprofit, you already know your job is to get the most high-quality mission that you can out the door every day by using *all the resources* of the organization. Here's the good news: "All the resources" in-cludes all the neurons of all the employees and volunteers of the organiza-tion. All of them. If you reach out and engage more people, if you explain what you need and ask people to get involved, if you tap the potential of each staff member and volunteer to improve your nonprofit in tiny, small, medium, and big ways, then your organization is doing collaborative innovation.

Collaborative innovation benefits from the wisdom of crowds, from the perspectives of many, from small, sometimes incomplete ideas that can be fleshed out by a group. It takes the weight off of leaders to be the only problem solvers and increases ownership throughout your nonprofit.

But, for many of us as leaders, this is harder than it looks. It takes time, patience, and a giving up of a certain level of control. It requires us to adopt two credos.

First and foremost: "Every idea is a good idea until we come up with the best idea, and the best idea does not have to be *my* idea." This is the lynchpin of being inclusive and making innovation safe (more on that in a bit), but the giving up, particularly for the CEO of the "my idea" part is very hard for many CEOs I've worked with.

 HANDS ON: Simply because CEOs are, well, the CEO, people often defer to their ideas. This means that leaders need to learn to speak last, not first, in innovation and idea sessions, that they need to applaud others' thoughts early and often, and, on a regular basis, say something like "I think you guys have covered it all, great!" and *not* add anything at the end of the discussion. This is *hard*, and I speak not only from watching CEOs make the adjustment, but from personal experience. ■

The second credo is this: "Put more neurons on the problem." This is another way of saying Chambers' credo of "No one of us is as smart . . . ." If you agree to try this, it means more asking and inclusion of everyone in your organization, not only staff, but governing and non-governing volunteers, the people you serve (and perhaps their families), your community, and your funders.

Peckham Innovation

Peckham has brought more and more and more neurons to the problems, and its managers credit this action for much of its success. "We've emphasized 'the value of the conversation'," notes Jo Sinha, Peckham's vice president. "We know that talking ideas through brings value and that, at the end of that conversation if we aren't passionate about an idea, if we don't have a manager who owns the idea, it won't move forward."

Peckham credits its move into higher-tech jobs to input in a town meeting from clients who wanted to move out of manufacturing work. It credits its new farm back to ideas from staff about developing community gardens—an idea that in turn grew from Peckham's focus on becoming a green organization.

Peckham also provides its staff with cash mini-grants to run with new ideas and test them out. It's intentional in seeking input from everyone. The result of course, is significant, but high-quality growth.

GING Innovation

Goodwill Industries of North Georgia (GING) encourages staff to develop ideas and values innovation in its programs. It's designed a format called an Issue Outline to make the process easier and faster. A staff person who has an idea shoots the outline to his or her supervisor and then follows the idea up the management chain. According to CEO Ray Bishop, "Ideas from our line staff and mid-managers have fueled our growth."

I've said for years that all the easy problems have been solved, and that most of the problems that remain have been outsourced to nonprofits. Why *wouldn't* we ask more people? Let's take a look at a pair of reasons.

We don't ask **the people we serve** because, well, we're the experts! And experts are supposed to know what's best. The problem there is that we don't view our services from the viewpoint of a service recipient because we can't. And anyway, what would we learn if we did?

 FOR EXAMPLE: A food bank in a large city in the northeast United States provided services in a fairly traditional way: It took food donations and asked its nutritionist to make up boxes of food that together provided healthy eating for recipients. Each week, the nutritionist did so with that week's donations and volunteers assembled boxes of food that were each identical. Recipients came in, took a small box if they were an individual and a larger box if they had a family, and left. Not an unusual way to provide the service and very efficient.

The food bank was popular, and growing. The staff and board touted the fact that each year, each quarter, "we're touching more lives," as measured by the number of boxes of food going out the door. All good, everyone's happy.

Until two local business-school students showed up asking to do a marketing assessment of the food bank as an internship. The food bank staff were thrilled; free marketing! Little did they know that the students were focused in their studies on end use, what customers actually *do* with the products they buy. Once the students had been oriented, they started watching what happened to the boxes after the recipients left the food bank. In some cases they asked recipients a quick survey, in some cases they were allowed to follow them home and look in their cupboards and refrigerators. In some cases they simply watched what happened.

And what happened was not at all what the staff, board, or nutritionist expected. Most of the food (more than 60 percent) was either never eaten or thrown away, sometimes in dumpsters within a block of the food bank. One of the students noted in the report, "I watched two people dump half their food in the dumpster within two minutes of leaving the food bank. A bit later, I went over and looked in the dumpster. It was a quarter full of food from the food bank. I immediately went in and got the executive director and brought him to take a look. He was stunned. Then he was resentful. Then he resolved to fix the problem."

Fixing the problem started with the staff asking the marketing students for their ideas. Since they were marketing students, they suggested asking the recipients for ideas. This caused immediate pushback from some of the staff, particularly the nutritionists. "They'll all just want the sugared cereal and drinks," or "C'mon, they're not going to pick healthy food."

The clear implication was that the recipients, since they were poor, weren't smart enough to contribute to the solution, and that the nutritionists should be in control. But the executive director (ED), to his credit, persisted and let the marketing students hold some focus groups with recipients to find out why people were throwing away food when they were hungry, and how the process could be improved to waste less food.

The results of the focus group were straightforward. The recipients, like the rest of us, prefer some foods over others. Some foods they really disliked, or, if they received the same kind of soup each week, were bored with. "Why can't we pick the food we get?" asked one. The ED noted that it was part of their job to make sure people ate balanced diets. One older woman piped up "I get that. We have to eat that pyramid thing. But that doesn't mean we can't pick our own food!" She was, of course, referring to the ubiquitous food pyramid, a picture of which was on the wall in the room where the focus group was being held.

The ED was silent (and later admitted he was stumped), but the marketing students asked the key question: "How do we do that?" The recipients kicked around a number of ideas and then came up with the solution: Organize the food choices into the pyramid. Let recipients choose one item from the top of the pyramid, two from the next level, three from the next, and so on.

This was a workable solution, but there was *still* resistance from the staff and volunteers. First, it would require a complete renovation of the pantry, with more shelving put in so that recipients could "shop" for their food. Second, it took away a key volunteer contribution, packing boxes of food. Third, it provided a risk that some donated food that was unpopular would not be used and would have to be thrown away.

(continued)

(continued)

But the ED persisted. He noted that the point of the food bank was to get more healthy food in people's stomachs, that they had data that more than half the food going out the door was being wasted, and that the point was not the work involved for staff, or the difficulty of using volunteers in a different way, but the mission outcome.

The result was a shopping experience for the recipients. Each food item is categorized and a colored sticker put on the box or can. Recipients know that they have to have two green items for every orange one, and two orange items for every blue one. They are checked out at the door to make sure their combinations of food are correct. Volunteers are used to stock the shelves correctly and to help with checkout. Food that is not popular is, when it nears its expiration date, transported to a nearby soup kitchen to be used to feed more people.

And, best of all, 90 percent of the food that goes out the door is actually consumed by recipients. Why? Because the recipient's perspective, the perspective ignored by the experts was right, and their solution worked. ■

We don't ask **staff, particularly new staff,** because we're the management team, we have more education, more experience than anyone else. If we can't solve a problem, how could they?

FOR EXAMPLE: Try this with your staff. Make copies of the figure below:

IX

Hand it out at a staff meeting and tell people *exactly* the following words:

"Take this, add one line, and turn this into a six."

Give the staff people 30 seconds or so to get the right answer. Perhaps one in 10 will. The answer, by the way, is:

SIX

I used to use this exercise to teach people to learn how to solve problems in different ways. But, in 1988, my then six-year-old son Benjamin was talking to me as I was preparing for a presentation. He was asking the age-old question, "What do you do at work, Daddy?" and I was trying my best to explain the job of management consultant and trainer in terms that he could understand.

I told him that, "I teach grownups." "Like in school?," he asked. "Yes, like that. I teach them things about where they work." "Do you play games?," he wanted to know. "Yes, sometimes," and as I said that I saw (and here's a blast from the past) a *transparency* that had the "IX" on it. Aha! A game!

"Benjamin," I said, showing him the IX. "Copy this." He did. "Now," I said, "take the pencil and with one line, turn this into a six." With no hesitation at all, he grabbed the pencil, added an "S" before the IX and said, "Like this?"

I was floored. I mean, I knew he was smart (*my* child and all that parental pride), but only about 10 percent of adults get this at all, much less immediately. What was going on?

What was going on, of course, was that Benjamin, as a first grader, had never learned about roman numerals. When he looked at an IX, he saw an "icks," not a "nine," which is what adults see. Adults see this as a math problem and couldn't come up with the solution. Ben saw it as a language problem—and solved it. In short, we, as adults have *too much information, too much education, too much knowledge* to solve this problem.

Later that week, I was visiting Benjamin's classroom, and I asked the teacher if I could repeat the activity with the class. Of 30 kids in the room, all 30 got it immediately.

The point here is, don't assume that because you have a college diploma or a masters or a doctorate or 20 years on the job that you can solve every problem better than someone without those degrees or experience. Sometimes you'll be *too smart, educated, or experienced to solve the problem.* ■

When you think of the IX remember this: What we *know* is often our biggest problem. You knew that was a nine, not an icks and thus couldn't find the solution. That's why asking more people is so powerful.

I noted earlier that collaborative innovation builds on the wisdom of crowds. That term is the title of the wonderful book by James Surowiecki on group and collaborative decision making. Surowiecki's base premise, backed up by data, is that one hundred randomly selected people will, in most cases, make a better decision or come up with a better solution to a problem than one or two experts. That means that the more we ask, the more useful things we learn. And, we build larger groups of people who are invested (because they gave us ideas) in what we're doing.

 HANDS ON: Technology is ready to help us here with wikis, Google Docs, online surveys, and instant feedback mechanisms. Asking lots of people on a regular basis does not always have to be time consuming or expensive. By the time you read this, there will be new and even more efficient ways of getting input. Your job as a leader is to accept the idea of asking more people, then ask your information technology (IT) staff or employees or volunteers who are tech savvy to come up with the best ways to do the asking. ■

One other generational note about collaboration: it plays directly into the training and work preferences of staff and volunteers who were born any time after 1975. Those of us born before that date were schooled individually; we took our tests, wrote our papers, did our science project alone. After 1980 (when the post 1975 birth year students would have started school) learning was taught much more collaboratively. They are comfortable in that environment. In fact, for staff and volunteers born after 1980, their school experience and technology allow them to socialize, date, volunteer, and donate to nonprofits, all in groups. Collaboration is their norm, and you might just want to involve these younger workers as you develop your collaborative innovation processes. They know how to do it.

Once again: Ask, ask more, be *overly* inclusive, and listen carefully.

Innovation Tools

There are countless books, webinars, and conferences on how to innovate, what to do to get the innovation spark going, how to become an innovator, and the like. A few of the really good ones are provided to you in the resources I list in the Appendix. What I want to do in this space is suggest a few seemingly mundane tools that you can use to spark more innovation. Some of what I'll suggest may not seem very edgy, but without using them, your nonprofit will just be doing more of the same thing you're doing now. Others are cutting edge and incredibly productive.

Keep Minds Flexible

One of the keys to innovation is to keep our minds flexible. As we age, all parts of our bodies become less flexible unless we work at it. This includes our minds. If we don't stretch minds regularly they become as creaky as our hamstrings. Stretching our minds is pretty simple, just pour new ideas in there regularly.

For you as a leader, this means to prioritize training, webinars, conferences for not just the senior management but for everyone. Most readers don't have to even leave town for good training. Your local community foundation or management service organization, or your state nonprofit association most likely provide excellent, regular training opportunities.

 HANDS ON: The next time you go to training, make sure you come back and review what you learned with your staff using language such as "Here's something I didn't know . . . , " or "Here's something we used to do that I think we should get back to . . . , " and "Here's something that was brought up that I'm not sure is for us, but what do you think?" The idea is to let your staff see that you know you don't know it all and to share what you heard as a basis for discussion. ■

Training and learning are key to the innovative organization. Assume that not everything people read, listen to, or are taught will be appropriate for your organization, but that's okay. Perhaps some of it will, and can be the basis for a new idea or improvement. Even if you reject all of what's proposed, it means you have to rethink and reaffirm what you're already doing.

Here are two other ways to pour ideas into people's heads on the cheap.

Book Clubs

Book clubs or reading groups are terrific ways to start discussions and to learn about your peers. Start with your management team and suggest they do the same with their direct reports. Pick three or four books (I have some suggestions in the Appendix for where to start) and read a chapter or two a month. Don't overwhelm people, particularly those who are not prone to read in their spare time. Get together over lunch, have a prepared set of discussion questions (open questions, like the ones at the end of every chapter in this book), and let the conversation flow. Don't dominate the discussion, and let everyone have their say. End every meeting with a question: In what we read, what can and should we apply to our organization?

You'll learn fascinating things about your staff doing this. You'll read Book A and assume that the big takeaway is X, and someone you thought you knew really well will read the same book and note that their big takeaway was not X, but an idea you had not even noticed. It's important for you to know more about your staffs' perspective on management, organizational improvement, and so on, and this is a quick look inside that perspective.

If you do this, don't be cheap. Buy copies (paper or digital) of the books you read for everyone. As someone who has facilitated book clubs for years for national nonprofits, you'd be amazed how much staff values the simple act of being given a book.

Field Trips

Remember how much you loved field trips in school? It got you out of the classroom and gave you a change of pace. You also learned something. Well, not that much has changed. The idea of field trips is to take mid-managers (who may not be sent out of town much) and set up site visits at other organizations like yours. They get out of the building, get to see what others are doing, and learn a ton.

The keys to this are as follows:

- First, send three people in a group. Not one, not two, not four, three. Make sure they are—to the extent practical—peers, not a supervisor and a couple of her direct reports. Also, it's better if you can offer this as an opportunity and take volunteers, but that may not be an option for you.

- Have them tour one or two or even three other organizations. (You'll have to set this up with your peer CEOs.) Make sure they get a tour and time to meet with their peers at the other organizations. This may well mean that they need to be gone overnight if your organization is in a small community. If so, pay for mileage, meals, hotel, and offer to pay for any child care needed.
- Tell them before they go what you expect them to look into, and even coach them on questions to ask. When they return, they should be expected to make a report to you and their peers of what they learned, and what could be applied at your nonprofit.

I've seen these kinds of experiences be huge growth events for mid-managers. They go off and find out that your nonprofit does really good work, but also see ideas from other organizations about how to be better. It helps them jump out of the rut of doing what you do the way you've always done it.

Try this once or twice and I suspect you'll have people lining up to be included in the next field experience.

Lead by Not Deciding

At least by not deciding everything and solving every problem. The more you do that, the more you allow your employees' problem-solving skills to get rusty. And you want them to solve problems. When someone comes to you and asks "What should we do about this, boss?" your first instinct is probably to give them an answer. It's better for them, and in the long run for you, to turn the question around and say "I'm interested in what *you* think the solution is." The staff person may not like that response (it's easier for them if *you* decide and also if things don't work out it's *your* fault not theirs), but be persistent. Then, if they come back with a reasonable solution (not perfect, and almost certainly not the same as you would have suggested) say "Sounds good to me, go with it."

This is a strategy that builds their confidence, forces them to think independently (or perhaps even ask others, building their own collaborative innovation network), and takes some of your load off. It's stressful, since you're letting go of the bicycle, but it's good leadership and staff mentoring.

HANDS ON: Once you start doing this with all your direct reports, you may want to make sure that they have a short checklist to weigh their solution/suggestion before they come in to talk to you. Something like this:

> *I love your ideas and your suggestions and am happiest when you bring me solutions to problems that confront us. I welcome them any time. That said, I want to lay out the way I'll be reviewing what you bring me, so that you can understand my criteria for evaluating things and, hopefully, adopt them as your own.*
>
> *— Does this idea support our mission? How?*
> *— Does this idea potentially violate any of our values? If so, how are you going to avoid that?*
> *— Do we have the resources (money, people, space, etc.) to implement this idea? If not, where do we get the needed resources?*
> *— Will doing this have a negative impact on the quality of services we provide?*
> *— Have you checked with others and gotten their input?*
>
> *Keep the ideas, suggestions, and problem solutions coming!* ■

Listen for Partial Ideas

Not all ideas come to you fully formed. I've often heard staff members or board members who will muse about an idea that you can tell is bouncing around in their heads but that they haven't fully fleshed out. This may be because they are hesitant about being made fun of, having their idea misunderstood, or that they simply want time to think it through more.

Be alert to these musings and short conversations. Encourage the board or staff member to keep talking. Ask them more about their idea, what prompted it, how it will help your nonprofit or its services. And, in some cases, you want to take the partially formed ideas (always WITH the person who first thought if it) to a larger group to brainstorm on. Which leads us to our final innovation tool.

Ask the Ignorant

This term, which came from an article on innovation in *Wired* magazine a few years back, is one I've fully adopted. It does not mean asking people who are, well, ignorant, but rather asking people who are not up to speed (i.e., ignorant) in your discipline. They could be your spouse or one of your children, your sister-in-law, your neighbor, or someone from your softball league.

While this may seem counterintuitive (what could *they* know about my problem?) to getting a good solution, it works on two levels. First, the ignorant don't know about your problem in all of its complexity and thus can often see a simpler, more direct solution than we can. Be alert here: The solution they come up with may be a partial one (see previous section) so listen carefully and keep an open mind.

The second outcome from asking someone who doesn't understand your business is that they don't understand your jargon. Thus, you have to describe your problem in what will seem like very basic terms, but in doing so *you* may well see a solution from a different angle yourself. I've had that happen to me on more than one occasion.

The moral here is that collaborative innovation can also be a one-on-one event, and that more neurons on the problem can, and should, include people outside of your discipline.

An Innovation/Problem-Solving Process

All of us know about brainstorming, which if well facilitated, can lead to a innovation frenzy around the seed of a good idea, even if that idea is only partially formed as we noted in the preceding section. But the best brainstorming sessions (and I've facilitated hundreds) do, in fact, start with one or more ideas. They aren't as great at generating new ideas as they are at improving existing ones. Brainstorming sessions also have two other flaws: Not everyone has to participate in the work of the session (they can sit there mute and not take any ownership) and there isn't the opportunity for all participants to see both sides of any solution, which, like participation, is key to ownership down the road.

Thus, I have become a huge fan of a process called **Pro-Con.** I've used it with dozens of groups over the past few years and I think it's a breakthrough in both group dynamics and collaborative problem solving.

In Pro-Con, you gather people into a room and have a facilitator, as you would for a strategic planning session. I suggest having at least 15 to 20 people in the room, and you can have as many as 50. The people in the room should be sitting at round tables, since they'll be working together. The rounds should be a minimum of six people and a max of eight.

Put the problem/issue on a flip chart or better, describe it in some detail in a handout. First, ask each person to take one minute (and only one) to write down a possible solution to the problem. NOTE: It's crucial that *everyone* does this. Next, ask each table to review the solutions at their table and to come to a consensus on the one or two they want to suggest to the room. That takes no more than 10 minutes.

Now, the facilitator goes around the room and has each table call out their solution or solutions. These are listed on a flip chart. Now, the entire group decides which solution to pursue first by a show of hands, applause, whatever works.

The facilitator should give the table (or person) who came up with the suggestion the opportunity to expand on the idea a bit to make sure everyone understands the idea.

Now, the fun starts. Split the room into two halves. Say you have 24 people sitting at rounds of six. That's four tables. Half (two tables) are told to take five minutes as a table and come up with all the reasons the selected idea will *not* work. This is the con side of the room. The other half, the pro side has the same five minutes to come up with all the positives they can think of regarding the idea.

When the five minutes are over, the facilitator asks each table to report its pros (or cons) and lists them on the flip chart.

And, now, we really shake things up. The facilitator gives all the pro tables five minutes to come up with new, different cons, and the con tables five minutes to come up with new, different pros. This is the best part of the exercise, and when it's done, the facilitator lists the new pros and cons.

And now, you send the groups back to improve the initial idea, using the pros and cons listed on the board.

You can do one round (as just described) or more of this exercise, but the process forces three things: Everyone has to participate, everyone (even those who might not normally speak up) gets the chance to support or oppose an idea, and everyone sees both sides of a solution.

 HANDS ON: I've just given you the thumbnail of Pro-Con. There's an entire workbook on this process available free online from The Center for Leadership Innovation. See the Appendix for more information on this tool as well as other books and papers. ■

Baking Innovation into the Organization

You may be a risk taker, an innovator, someone who likes the new, is what's called an *early adaptor* in the tech world, someone who is not afraid of failing if they learn something. "Nothing ventured, nothing gained" might be one of your mottos.

That's great, and all good characteristics in a leader as long as the risk you take is overlaid with good decision and business skills. But there is no question in my mind that part of Smart Stewardship is taking reasonable risk on behalf of the people you serve.

But the truth is, not everyone feels the way you do. Some people like the status quo. It's comfortable, non-risky, and they would have to face up (to themselves or their supervisors) if their innovation ideas don't work out perfectly. They may have grown up in an environment where their ideas or suggestions were derided, or their first boss may have told them to shut up one too many times. They've become risk averse.

Remember Exhibit 7.1, the bell curve we saw earlier regarding innovations? Take a look at it again and imagine it in the light of trying to get more people in your organization to be innovative.

On the left of our new curve, you would see that a small group is never going to participate in your innovation culture. They'll sit on the sideline and watch (which is why Pro-Con is so great—they *have* to participate), not have any ownership, and eventually resent the changes. With these people, your job is to erode their numbers to the minimum, knowing you'll never get everyone.

The far right of the curve is full of people who came to work ready to posit their ideas, try new things, and may or may not have been able to up until now if you haven't been practicing collaborative innovation. These are the people whose enthusiasm you need to encourage and reinforce, then step back and let them run. They'll be awesome, and their enthusiasm will draw in people from the middle group in the curve.

Speaking of that large bulge in the center, this group is the one you have to cajole, help along, practice patience with, and make sure that innovating is safe for. They are what we might term innovation fence sitters, and your job is to get them to voluntarily step off the fence and become more engaged.

Because you need all the help you can get to solve the problems and crises that face your nonprofit. You've already seen the benefits of asking more people more often, even those who you might have thought had nothing of value to contribute. But surveys and focus groups, Pro-Con sessions, and suggestion boxes only go so far. You have to bake innovation into your organization. This takes some time, and certainly takes leadership. Here's how.

Make Innovating and New Ideas as Safe as Possible

Remember the mantra we looked at earlier in this chapter: *Every idea is a good idea until we come up with the best idea, and the best idea doesn't have to be my idea.* If you act on that, you'll welcome every idea, and that means even the crazy ones. If you're leading an idea session, and you hear an idea that you know won't work, and even smirk, much less laugh or snort or give any disparaging sound, you've just given a loud warning to all those fence sitters that this activity is not safe, and that they are better off staying put on the fence.

You have to not only lead this, but you must, must, *must* train your supervisors to practice it with their direct reports, and hold them accountable. The best innovations usually come from the people closest to the line of service. You need the direct line supervisors to be enabling new thoughts and ideas. Tell people you will not tolerate sarcasm about someone's suggestion. Remember that value you probably have on the wall, *respect.* Tell your supervisors to practice it!

If you can make the environment safe for suggestions, you've made a huge start on developing your innovation culture.

Embrace Innovations That Are Not Yours

The next leadership challenge is to embrace (not merely tolerate) ideas that are someone else's. Again, this is hard for some of us who have been the innovators and problem solvers for so many years. But, to make the transition into an innovation culture, you have to show that ideas other than yours are not only considered, but chosen when they merit it.

 HANDS ON: The sooner you can find and celebrate an idea that comes from the line of service or close to it, the better. If you, as CEO or a senior manager, are seen as not only buying in to the innovation, but strongly supporting it, that message goes a long way. Remember, when noting (and hopefully touting) the idea to say things like "I never could have come up with that idea," or "This shows why we count on the staff at the line of service to show us the way." Verbalize what people need to hear. ■

 HANDS ON: If you have a set of solutions to choose from, some yours, some from others, and those choices are relatively even in risk or likely outcome, choose the subordinates' ideas whenever possible. This is also a clear message that you're listening. ■

 HANDS ON: Sometimes you have to force the issue. We talked about this situation earlier, but let's recap: When a staff person comes to you and says something to the effect of "What do you want to do about X, boss?" your answer should almost always be "What do you think we should do?," even if the solution is obvious to you. You may even need to send them away to come back with an idea or solution, and when they do, unless their idea is a felony, or will put people or the organization in danger, go with it. *Even if you think it will fail* (see the next step). ■

Remember That Some Innovations Will Fail (and That's Okay)

Doing new stuff, changing the way you do things now, trying something another organization has developed, it's all risky to some extent. There *will* be failures and setbacks. That's how we learn. If your subordinate in the *hands on* example earlier comes up with an idea and you tell them "sounds good to me," you're doing what we said earlier has to happen for people and organizations to grow: You're letting go of the bicycle. It's hard, scary (for the subordinate and you, at least at first), but rarely disastrous. If things go wrong, what do you do? Look at the next step.

Celebrate the *Attempts* as Well as the *Successes*

Someone, we'll call him Tom, works for you. He takes the idea of all this innovation stuff to heart and tries something new. It doesn't work. In fact, it crashes and burns. Now, you have two basic ways to respond.

One is to get up in his face and yell: *"Tom, what is wrong with you? What were you thinking?!?!"*

How soon do you think Tom will try something again? Not in this life. And neither will his peers or anyone else who witnesses (or hears about) your put down. Now they are no longer fence sitters, but have walked away from the fence to join the totally risk-averse group.

Or, you could say to Tom and his peers something like this, *"Tom tried to improve things by doing___. As we all know, it didn't work out as we all had hoped. We've all been where Tom is. What can we learn from this?"*

This way, everyone learns from Tom's mistakes, and mistakes become, if not celebrated, at least okay.

Trust me, taking the second option is *hard*. But I learned as a supervisor and deputy director that yelling just shut down innovation. Slowly, I adjusted my attitude, and by the time I was CEO, I had begun to go by what anyone who ever worked for me knew was the "Primary Rule of Working for Peter": *Make any mistake you want. Once.*

This rule enabled the wonderful people who I worked with to try, mess up, back up, and try again. But if you congratulate people for the attempt, commiserate with them and share with everyone what you've learned, you'll grow your staff and your organization.

Be Patient

Any cultural change, and that's really what we're talking about, starts with changing behaviors. And those always take longer than we'd like. It will take time for the risk averse to move from the left-hand side of the bell curve in Exhibit 7.1 to the center or even center right. People will wait and see what happens the first time (and second time and third time) that an *innovation* doesn't work. That's why it's so important that you lead from the front.

People will also feel their ideas are not worthy of bringing up, or that they'll wait to give you the idea until they've "thought it through a bit more." Be patient and understanding.

Finally, when people do give you ideas, they'll want to know what happened to them. Were they used, discarded, put aside, or rejected? If you don't tell them what happened, the idea well will dry up.

Reward Carefully

While you certainly should reward successful innovations that improve your organization's mission capability, make sure you do it carefully. It's not unusual for managers to create reward systems and incentives that they, the managers value, but are either not desirable or, worse, resented by the people they are supposed to reward. Certainly you want to note big moves forward, but you also don't want to ignore the people who do the little innovations that also improve mission capability. Think this through carefully. Should there be public awards? Some people love public recognition and some *hate* it. Should there be a component on every staff person's evaluation about their innovations? If so, how do you measure it? Tread carefully here.

Only by baking innovation into your organizational culture can you assure that the most people possible will be both contributing ideas themselves as well as coaching up the next generation of staff and volunteers. It takes time, patience, and steady leadership, but without going through the process, you will, at best, get a temporary spike in ideas, creativity, and innovation and then return to the old, non-innovation norm.

Recap

In this chapter, I've shown you how to make constant, steady, and collaborative innovation the norm in your nonprofit. We started by looking at the issue of why people see innovation as so hard. I told you that not only do we all innovate all the time, that the key is not looking for huge leaps forward, but regular steady small innovations and building a habit of trying new things, an environment that makes experimentation safe, and a culture that values the new. I showed you that only a tiny minority of innovations are really the Eureka! variety, but that improvements in your services and administrative functions can lead to a better, more mission-focused organization.

Then we turned to collaborative innovation, which is, in my opinion, the best way to start to get innovation as the norm in your organization. We discussed how collaboration not only taps more of the staff and volunteer experience that you already have, but also generates more ownership within those same groups and particularly appeals to younger workers and volunteers, who were trained in collaboration throughout their school years.

I next showed you some innovation tools and resources including the need to keep minds more flexible by offering training, book clubs, and field trips, as well as the need for you and the senior management to share their training experiences regularly. I told you about how to jump start more innovation by not deciding, but rather by throwing back the decisions to the people you supervise, and how listening better can alert you to ideas that only come to you partially formed.

We then spent a bit of time with the process called Pro-Con, which I think has huge potential to unlock groups from traditional thinking and to develop interesting and innovative solutions to vexing problems.

Finally, I showed you how to bake innovation into your organization by making it a priority. Again, we reviewed the vital concept and attitude that "Every idea is a good idea until we find the best idea, and the best idea does not have to be my idea." This attitude will lead into all the rest of my suggestions, which were:

- Make innovating and new ideas as safe as possible.
- Embrace innovations that are not yours.
- Remember that some innovations will fail. And that's okay.
- Celebrate the *attempts* as well as the *successes*.
- Be patient.
- Reward carefully

Remember, only by innovating constantly can you fulfill any values you might have of being world class or best in the field. Only by innovating collaboratively can you fulfill my definition of a steward, which is someone who uses "*all* the resources of the organization," which include, of course, the brains, experience, and perspectives of each and every staff member and volunteer. Only by baking innovation into the organization can you assure that a culture of constant innovating will continue long after you leave the organization.

So now you know how to draw on more resources and work on getting more valuable innovations out the door on a regular basis. You've seen the Smart Stewardship decision tree, and know how to use that tool, and hopefully customize it for your own organization. You know about mission, values, competence, capacity, cash, and quality and how they play into the decision-making process. You're set to move ahead.

But wait, there are two more subjects we haven't discussed, or at least have only touched on, and they are the subject of the final two substantive chapters of this book: Chapter 8, Going to Scale and Chapter 9, Smart Stewardship in Good Times and Bad. Going to scale is an all-too-loud call from many funders, but that doesn't mean it shouldn't happen for some nonprofits, perhaps including yours. We'll look at how to evaluate your ability to go to scale and what the costs and benefits are.

Finally in Chapter 9, I'll show you how to be a Smart Steward all the time, even when things turn sour, funding reduces, or a crisis rears its head. I'll give you a checklist of things to remember and some strategies for getting through the dark times, which show up when we least expect them. The good news is that, as a Smart Steward, you'll be ready when those bad times arrive.

Discussion Questions

1. How do we *really* treat ideas from people other than the management team? Do we really believe that every idea is a good idea until we find the best idea? And is our idea always the best idea?
2. How can we develop more ideas and use more people to do so?
3. Should we develop an innovation idea filter to help people and lower-level managers sort through ideas?
4. Do we need to add "innovation" as a value? If we do, can we at the management level live up to it?
5. What can or should we do about recognizing and rewarding innovation?
6. What's our next step in this all-important area?

CHAPTER 8

Going to Scale

Chapter Thumbnail

Overview

As this book is being written, the mantra of "going to scale" is everywhere in the nonprofit sector. It's the current big thing for funders to demand and, at its core is very, very dangerous for many nonprofits. Why? Because it pushes nonprofits, often desperate for funding, to only apply for funds for programs that can grow quickly. You've just finished reading about the high cost of rapid growth, about doing more of what you do well, about outreaching your capacity, and all of those rules are broken when a foundation or governmental or corporate funder demands a quick move up to scale.

That said, expanding your services or expanding one core service significantly can be a solid move for a mission-based organization. Obviously, some nonprofits are already huge, with multiple sites in multiple locations, hundreds, if not thousands of staff and volunteers doing wonderful mission. But they didn't get that way by chance, or overnight.

Many large nonprofits grew organically: Slowly, over many years. Others made a faster leap, making the decision to grow quickly. Some chose the franchise model, some not. Some ceded local control of their idea, some

127

wanted to retain that control. Some succeeded, and some abandoned the growth idea after meeting obstacles they couldn't overcome.

Let's take a minute to define what it is we're talking about. As with all trendy terms, going to scale is used in a variety of ways, so let's get a single definition to use.

Going to scale (or scaling up, as it is also called) in the social sector means "*Institutionalizing* programs in a way that allows you to reach more of a target audience, usually in a larger geographic area." The term actually comes from manufacturing, where making large numbers of a product often results in economies of scale that make the company profitable. That's great for manufacturing, but the same economies don't show up for organizations where the vast majority of expenses are employee centered.

That said, the key word in the definition is institutionalizing. That clearly implies making a service replicable throughout the institution, or the sector. That's hard.

In this chapter, we'll examine the idea of going to scale, what it entails, some models, and, no surprise, some cautions.

We'll start by looking at the key question of whether your mission-provision methods can be duplicated at a high level of quality elsewhere. If you can't do this, you can't scale.

Next, we'll look at another overused term: models. How often have you heard a funder, or a board member, or someone at a conference say something like: "This organization is a model for all of us"? Sounds good, but the truth on the ground is a bit different.

Then we'll turn to the issue of reasonable growth curves. If you do intend to make a large growth effort, what's reasonable to plan, what's reasonable to fund? We'll take a look at some ideas and some experiences. After this, we'll look at the key question of investment options: how much time, talent, and treasure do you want to invest in this growth effort?

Next, a marketing question: Does the market want what you are offering? You'd be amazed how many organizations (for profit and non-profit) go into a new community without researching that make-or-break question.

With those questions answered, we can talk about different ways to scale. Franchising, open source, seed planting, and other methods will be discussed. And, to close the chapter, I'll give you a checklist to use if you make the decision to go to scale.

Is scaling risky? Yes. It is *not* for many nonprofit organizations. But if it is for you, it offers great mission opportunities. By the end of the chapter, you should be able to see whether this is a good strategy to consider or one to avoid, at least for the time being.

Can Your Mission-Provision Methods Be Duplicated?

Think about nonprofits that are *everywhere*. To do that, think of the high-value nonprofit brands, ones like Habitat for Humanity, Goodwill Industries, Susan G. Komen, the YMCA, Girl Scouts, Ronald McDonald House Charities (RMHC). Why are they everywhere? Because they're rich? Because they had unlimited resources?

No. These iconic nonprofits are everywhere because they have a very good, easily understandable core idea, one that motivates people to say "Hey, we should do that here," *combined* with a methodology that can be understood and then replicated with local customization, *combined* with terrific national support and structure.

 FOR EXAMPLE: What's the core idea of a Goodwill Industries? The business model is to have people donate goods, sell them in an appealing retail location, and use the profits to fund other jobs-related programs. Formed in 1902 in Boston, Goodwills now work in every part of the United States and Canada as well as 15 other nations.

How about the YMCA? Originally formed to provide safe, Christian housing for young men moving to large cities, the Y has spread and evolved with the times. Today, the mission is to strengthen the mind, body, and spirit of the community. You might argue that the Y focuses mostly on the "body" part of that triad, but over 200 years, they've become an institution in the United States.

On a shorter timeline since its founding in 1967, so has Habitat for Humanity, based again, on a simple, appealing replicable idea: Use volunteers to work alongside the eventual owner to construct housing.

Ronald McDonald House? Let's provide a place for the families of critically ill children to stay at no cost. Susan Komen? Let's find a cure for breast cancer, a type of cancer that affects nearly every family in the United States.

All simple, appealing ideas that are replicable locally. ■

Now, what about your scaling idea? If you really want to go to scale, if you really want to make a huge regional, national, or global mission impact, heck, if you simply want to open four more branches in your local county, you have to have a simple, replicable idea that takes into account local needs, wants, and cultures.

If you're thinking about scaling up, how are you going to teach others how to do what you've done? Will you write it down, put a series of videos on YouTube, develop a training program, how? Choose one or more, because you can't be everywhere, and your top staff can't all go off into the field and leave your current service area bereft of expertise.

So, the first question is this: Is our idea, our service, truly replicable? Can it be done well by others the way we do it? Just because *you* can do your mission well doesn't mean that others can. Just because *you* get what makes your nonprofit special, doesn't mean the exact same thing will happen the exact same way elsewhere.

In fact, that's the secret . . . it won't. In every new community, in every new location, your mission provision, if it's successful, will have to adapt. More precisely, you'll have to design a mission-replication system that is adaptable, that is *flexible* enough to accommodate needed modifications on the ground.

FOR EXAMPLE: Ronald McDonald House Charities (RMHC) provide shelter and food for the families of critically ill children in hundreds of locations in 53 countries (as of this writing), starting with the first house in 1974 in Philadelphia. Are all houses the same? No, of course not. Not only do the houses vary in design and size, some of the local 501(c)(3)s that run them also provide what are called Family Rooms (located right in the hospital) and/or Care Mobiles that provide needed care in the community.

The idea is simple: Housing for the families of critically ill children. The idea is replicable, but varies by location. A national, then international organization sprang up to guide, educate, and support the locals. And RMHC went to scale with a speed and breadth (and success rate) not often seen in the nonprofit world.

Your scaling plans may be just as ambitious, or a bit more down to earth, but the central question remains: Is our success based on the way we provide service, or the special people who provide it? Could we plug in our process with any group of great people, is our provision excellence really an outgrowth of who we are?

The answer to this question will guide your next decision: At your other locations, are you going to replicate *process* (and let culture develop) or are you going to replicate your *culture* first and then overlay the process?

FOR EXAMPLE: Peckham is fully in the "we export our culture" camp. They feel that if they can start by having everyone organization wide on the same culture page, the rest of the services and their quality will fall into place. In a long conversation with the senior management team, I pushed them about process over culture as they expand and there was a unanimous opinion that culture had to lead. "The people who come to work here (and will come to work in our other locations), we want them to share the same values, have the same benefits of working that we do. We start with embedding our culture into a new location." ■

Other nonprofits have successfully exported process, the sequence of events that lead to mission output. Habitat for Humanity has done this well. Of course, at the local level, Habitat overwhelmingly uses volunteers who may only work on one or two house builds. They don't have large (in some cases any) local staff. Thus, if Habitat led with culture, they'd constantly be behind the curve. So, process first.

Finally, as you think about whether your mission is replicable, you'll begin to use the term model, as in "We could be a model . . . ," or "What's our model of service?," or "Are there other scaling models we could adapt?" That's pretty normal, and it makes it a great time to look at the truth about models.

The Truth about Models

Models are time savers. Models are traps. Models can get you jump started to do more mission and can bog you down in a quicksand of perceived failure where others succeeded. Models are another tyranny of funders right now: "We only fund projects that can go to scale and become a model for other nonprofits" is a line I hear or read all the time.

Thus, models need to be looked at harder and considered in the full light of what they really are. Let's start with smaller, more common models and work up to models of service practice.

The old adage about not reinventing the wheel has application here: If someone else is doing something awesome in our area of mission, why not just copy what they do? Makes sense to me, and I regularly tell my clients, particularly when developing policies and procedures, to review what's online, what's available from peer organizations, and what is considered best practice. A bit of cut and paste and you're done, right?

Not so much. With policies and procedures, you need to look at what others have done and take the parts that work for you, that work within your value structure, that will work for the culture you've so carefully developed. If you simply adopt a policy wholesale, you risk violating your values and damaging all that you've worked for—not smart. Thus, carefully vetting what others have done (as always, with lots of neurons on the problem) will assure you get the best possible product at the end, probably from multiple sources.

HANDS ON: When reviewing policies to develop your own, make sure you use not only senior managers and board members, but staff and volunteers who will actually implement the policy or be personally affected by the document. I've seen chief financial officers (CFOs) create financial-reporting policies without asking for input from their financial staff, the people who actually have to process the information.

More importantly, though, when you start the process of document review (looking at existing models) ask those same line staff for anything they've seen online, or in other organizations, or in classes (assuming you're a true life-long learning organization). By taking their input from the start, you'll get better ideas and more ownership. ■

And you thought it was going to be much, much easier than writing from scratch!

In truth, it is faster and more focused, but it's not quick. The temptation to read a policy and say, "Yep, this will work; we're good," is *huge* when you have lots to do and not enough time to do it. But the value of using others' work as a starting point is just that; it's a starting point, not an end all.

So it is with service models, but with an additional trap: Any model, no matter how awesome, is only as good, only as replicable as the people who are assigned to adopt it. Thus, if a funder, or board member, or staff member comes to you and says "Hey, Nonprofit X has developed this cool model of service delivery. Let's do what they've done!," you have a whole bunch of questions to ask before going on, and most of them are in our decision tree: Does it support mission? Does it support (or violate) our values? Are we good at this? Do we have the capacity (including a champion), and enough cash? Finally, in doing your business plan/feasibility study, will what worked for Nonprofit X in Nonprofit X's community work for you? And, most importantly, do you have the right person doing the actual work?

 FOR EXAMPLE: After college, I did two tours as a Volunteers in Service to America (VISTA) volunteer. In my first job, I was a paramedic, working with two nurses to start a health clinic in a town of 500 people in rural Louisiana. I had worked as a medic in the Emergency Room (ER) of the Hospital of the University of Pennsylvania all four years as an undergraduate, and had tons of ideas on how to grow the clinic. Since the ER was in an achingly poor neighborhood, we did immunizations, well-baby clinics, STD counseling, and the like all right in the ER, because there was no other primary care location for many blocks. I'd seen how that had succeeded, so I thought I was good to go.

But over and over, I learned that my experiences in a poor neighborhood in Philadelphia were not easily transferrable to a poor community in the rural South. It was incredibly frustrating, since I *knew* what worked, and couldn't understand why I was failing.

In VISTA training, before being sent into the field, we were given four or five ways (read: models) to do community organizing or affect change. The trainers told us that we had to go slow, be flexible, gain trust, and customize what we were doing for each community. I heard them, but I only had a year to save the world (the standard VISTA service term), and I knew the model I wanted to use had worked elsewhere.

But it didn't work in rural Louisiana in 1975. Why? Because I was the wrong person to implement it. I was too much in a rush, too sure of myself, unwilling to take the time to gain trust: I felt people should just believe me.

The model was fine. The person implementing it wasn't. ∎

Make sure if you're pushed to use someone else's model, you look at what they do in depth. For example, what's the core success factor of Habitat for Humanity? Having volunteers build the home? Having the materials donated? Having the eventual resident work alongside the volunteers? Incredible project-management skills? Incredible volunteer-management skills? Something else that's invisible to outsiders?

You see, the Habitat model is widely known: Have volunteers work side-by-side with the person they're building a house for. Simple, cool, and harkens back to the days of communities coming together to raise a barn. But to implement the idea, the core competence needed is a *very* specialized kind of organizational skill: construction management *with volunteers*. If you don't have that, the model, which is simple and appealing, can't be duplicated.

Or, let's look at Goodwill Industries donated-goods-store model. Great idea, and how hard can it be? You get people to donate stuff, put it on a shelf, employ the people you're trying to help to work there, and use the profits to fund other programs. This model, which actually was the genesis of the Goodwill movement, is seductively simple. And, it's been copied by other nonprofits, but with widely varying success, while Goodwill stores nationwide, run by more than 100 different local Goodwills are consistently profitable and employ thousands of people. Why?

Because Goodwill seeks to find the best possible retail talent to manage the model. The model is great, but the right person or people with the right skillset makes it possible.

So, if you're pushed to use a model, don't forget to do your drill down homework. If possible, visit others who have succeeded with the model and ask detailed questions about what worked, what didn't, and what the core competencies are that make the model feasible. And put more neurons on the problem.

What's a Reasonable Growth Curve?

I am regularly asked about how fast an organization can grow over a sustained period without overtaxing itself. The best analogy I can give you is running.

 FOR EXAMPLE: Think of the difference between sprinting and running long distances. In both events you have to be in shape before you start. Sounds obvious, but is your organization in shape, ready to grow?

Next, you can only run fast for so long. I "ran" track in high school and college (actually I was a hammer thrower, so running was not a big part of my repertoire, but that's what they call it), and I was always most impressed with people who ran the long sprints, not the 100- or 200-meter dashes, but the 400 and 800. Those athletes ran really fast for a really, really long time. And, after the race I would see many more of them on the ground gasping for air than I saw the 100-meter people collapse. Why? You can't sustain a sprint for too long without overtaxing the systems. ■

So it is for you and your nonprofit. The first question is, of course, are you "in shape"? This means, do you have the management depth, the board skillset, the back office capacity, and, of course, the cash to grow?

If you're good there, then remember, you're not talking just about growth, or even rapid growth. In this chapter we're talking about scaling, which usually means growing really fast. What's really fast? Doubling your size in five years is really fast. For most organizations, frankly, it's unsustainable. But I know some that have set it as a goal. Some have succeeded, more have failed, but let's look at what that takes.

In terms of percentages, it means you roughly grow at 15 percent every year for five years (the compounding takes care of the difference). For most organizations, it won't be a straight 15 percent per year, though. Some years will be 5 percent, some 30 percent. And, at some point in the growth race, you simply have to take a break, rest, and catch up.

In long-distance running, you're taught to run intervals during your training runs. Thus, you might go out to run 5 miles and run it at a relatively slow pace of say eight-and-a-half minutes a mile. Every mile, though, you run about 200 meters much faster, at a seven-minute-mile pace, then return to your slower speed. It's a way to get stronger and faster, but can only be sustained for so long. I've run lots of intervals, and you have to slow down to let your body recover before you can speed up again, no matter how good a shape you are in.

And that's my advice if you're thinking about scaling. Have periods of slow growth interspersed with fast growth. If you're going to open a second or third or fourth location, don't open all of them in the same 18-month period. Spread the openings out, allowing your organizational system to catch up and breathe a bit. Then grow again when you've caught your collective breath.

There is, of course, no perfect pace of growth, and the term *reasonable* is completely subjective. What's reasonable is dependent on your readiness, your willingness to take risk, your management skill, your board support, and your cash flow. Just remember that with well-intentioned enthusiasm to expand your mission you can exceed your cash, quality, and capacity and wind up like those 800-meter runners; collapsed, unable to stay standing.

How Much Time, Talent, and Treasure Do You Want to Invest?

In the Smart Stewardship decision tree, look at decision point number six. "Have we done the appropriate business analyses?" To answer the question of how much time, talent, and treasure you want to invest (which, by the way, is a board/senior staff decision) you simply *must* do a business plan. Not some slap-dash, three-page review, not just a spreadsheet (no matter how detailed), not just an outline of the idea: you need a full-bodied, robust business plan.

You have to do the research, look for what can go wrong, examine the key factors of success (like the construction-management skills for Habitat), do your market research (see the section that follows on market research) and, of course, run the numbers. Do. Not. Proceed. Without. A Business Plan.

 HANDS ON: There are many good business-plan samples online for nonprofits, but you might also think about getting some outside consulting help for this work, from someone who has taken other businesses up to scale. I know outsiders are expensive, but this is a huge risk for the organization, and spending money now can both prevent disaster and smooth some bumps down the road. ■

Before I get into the specifics of time, talent, and treasure, remember, *how* you scale is going to be key. Remember what I told you earlier, you can scale primarily by *process* or scale primarily by *culture*. If you go the culture route, the costs are almost all higher across the board, but the mission outcomes may well be more lasting. That's really the first decision to make when you think about scaling: culture or process?

With that said, let's look at some things you might not have considered in the time-talent-treasure area.

Time

Growth, particularly rapid growth, is a black hole for time. Management time, board time, volunteer time are all sucked into supporting growth. As you look at your daily work load, do you have two to three hours extra each day to dedicate to scaling? Can you add an hour to every board meeting for the next three years to deal with issues of scaling, both before you decide to grow and after you initiate the growth? These numbers may sound silly, but they're not—they're real numbers given to me by chief executive officers (CEOs) and board members of organizations that have decided to scale up.

Remember, even though you decide to scale, you still have to manage your existing organization. And, the truth is, growth is seductive, drawing you away from attention to detail on what's already in place, keeping you from focusing on quality of service, or on innovating in the community you're currently serving. That's a time cost as well.

Talent

So, you're going to scale. Who do you ask to be your champion? Your slacker staff? No, of course not, you put your best people on the task. How does that affect your current services, and their current level of quality?

 FOR EXAMPLE: I recently had dinner with the CEO and chief operating officer (COO) of a large nonprofit based in the Puget Sound. The organization has been expanding services to other states, and had just been given an opportunity to set up an operation in Arizona. I asked Jeff, the CEO, how he had decided who to send down to the desert to run the new outpost. "We looked at our five best managers, matched their skills with the skills needed to be both a site manager and on their own, and came down to Tom. We asked him and he jumped at the chance. But we have very, very specific outcomes for Tom to meet, and we've sent him to spend a few days with the managers of each of our other remote locations to learn from their experiences. He'll do fine."

Then the COO jumped in: "But he'll be really, really tough to replace, and the area he manages here is crucial to our continued success. I'm really concerned about losing Tom here in Seattle." ■

In a nutshell, that's the issue: You'll send your best people off to another community to be your champion. If you're like most nonprofits, you're already under-managed, and don't have a deep bench. What will the effect be on quality, on the other managers left behind, on the program that your "Tom" ran? Key questions to consider.

Treasure

You know, from reading Chapter 6, that growth sucks up cash like a giant vacuum cleaner. Remember my example of the "free, no risk" $1,000,000 grant that cost $204,000 in cash to afford? In that example, funds were coming in after 75 days. In a new location, or a large expansion, no such financial cavalry may be riding over the hill to save you for many months, even years.

So, run the numbers, and run them conservatively. That's a key part of any business plan. As a steward, you also need to look at what's called the "opportunity cost" of that money; what you would do with the funds if they weren't going into your scaling. This is more than just the interest the funds might earn if you kept the cash invested. Much more important is what mission use you would put the funds to if you *didn't* scale, what mission flexibility you are losing if you put all your cash into rapid growth, and what loss of stability you have if other areas of your mission work go bad.

 FOR EXAMPLE: Imagine it's 2006, the height of the most recent good economic times. Say your nonprofit had decided on a growth path and opened two new offices in adjoining states. You invested 95 percent of your cash reserves doing this and the new outposts are doing fine. The business model is state-funded services, and your particular service model has great outcomes at a reasonable cost, something very attractive to any funder.

Now, 2008 comes along and let's say your home office (and funding streams) are in California, or Illinois, two of the states that financially seized up first in the recession. The state funding at your home base is cut 20 percent and your reserves are mostly gone, spent on an expansion to other states which for the moment are hanging on to their budgets, but in the next 18 months will all suffer huge budget cuts. You are suddenly in a very hard place next to a very big rock.

You made a good mission decision to expand. The new locations are successful, doing great mission. You researched and wrote a good business plan. But in spending nearly all of your reserves, you ate up your flexibility.

(continued)

(*continued*)

Remember what I told you about cash? That *cash equals oxygen*. Moreover, in a crisis, just like oxygen, cash on hand buys you time; time to think, time to adjust, time to make Smart Stewardship decisions. ■

If you decide to scale, remember to not only go through our Smart Stewardship decision tree, but to pay special attention to the ripple effect that your investments of time, talent, and treasure have. These are weighty, board- and senior staff-level topics.

Finally, scaling can be a way to bring lots of mission to lots of people. And that's good. Before I show you how some other nonprofits have successfully scaled, we have to deal with a crucial marketing question: Do people really want what you're going to scale?

Does Your Market Really Want What You Have to Offer?

If you do want to grow quickly, if you do want to scale, if you do have a replicable program and the cash, time, and talent to implement then you're good, right?

Hold on. I've already referred repeatedly to the decision point on the Smart Stewardship decision tree that reads: "Have we done the appropriate business analyses?" This will mean at least a feasibility study and most likely also a business plan, because going to scale is a huge strategic decision with immense risks. You'll run the numbers, look at outcome measures, list goals and objectives, but before all of that, you should ask this question: *Does the community we're providing mission to (our market) want what we're providing, in the way that we're providing it, for the price (if any) that we're providing it, at the time and location we're providing it?*

If the answer to that question (and all of its components) is not a resounding "Yes!", no matter how cool the model, the scaling is doomed. You have to investigate each different market's wants (not needs, wants) as part of your business planning. This is called a market analysis and it will be an essential part of the difference between success and failure of any scaling program. You can put aside sufficient cash, pick the perfect person to implement, and be willing to put up with initial losses of time and talent, but if your market is not interested in your service, or interested in the service the way you're providing it, the game's over.

Thus, you need to ask, in the community you're expanding to. You need to ask potential users, community leaders, other nonprofits, and, of course your staff who may already live there. Ask, ask, ask, and then listen!

Note: for much more on marketing and market analysis see my book *Mission-Based Marketing, Third Edition* (Wiley, 2010).

You may be enamored of your services. You may be justifiably proud of their success, and your organization's innovation. But remember this: What we're proud of is sometimes not what others see as good service, and if they don't *want* what we're providing, we aren't going to be doing much mission.

To this point, I've given you lots to think about. Now, let's look at some models (ironic, right?) of ways nonprofits scale.

Models for Scaling

Now that the key questions about scaling are rolling around in your head, what are the choices you have if you want to proceed? What have other nonprofits done? How have they done it? What are the models, methods, and structures they've used? There are many, so many that you could almost develop a second decision tree for how to scale. But it would be a short tree, because there are really only two questions.

The first question on this reduced decision tree might surprise you: **How much control do you want of the scaling?** Does your board (or management team) feel that tight control is essential to see that the mission is done properly? That's fine, but costs more money, time, effort, and liability.

Or, can you give up some control and put the idea in the hands of others? If so, less time, money, and oversight are needed. Or, is your need for control somewhere in between? The choice of level of control comes first. That's the strategic issue.

The second decision is more tactical. **What mechanism will you use to scale?**

Are you planning on *opening more offices* under your current 501(c)(3)? That would result in complete control: control of staff, budget, office location, decor, branding, and so on. A bit less control would come from a *subsidiary model,* where you open or take over another local 501(c)(3) in a remote community. There could be a local board overseeing a local staff. Perhaps the local gets budget approval from your organization, perhaps not. Perhaps your board has representation on the subsidiary board, perhaps not. A third option would be for you to *brand and deliver,* developing a how-to guide on a web site, but to copyright the idea and trademark the brand. This might bring you some funds, but more importantly it would give you some control of the way the idea is used in other communities. You could set standards to go along with use of the brand name, offer on-site consulting, and so on.

The least control comes from simply floating the idea, with your experience and a set of suggested processes. I call this the *open source* option, named after the very common software model, where programmers develop code, either in snippets, or in complete programs, and then put them online for others to use and/or improve. Nonprofits already do this for things like policies and procedures, and web sites such as IdeaEncore.com have led the way in facilitating the free exchange of documents. In your case, you would not just share a document, but an entire service concept.

Just remember that once a programmer posts open source code online, anyone is free to use it and, more importantly, to modify it. The original programmer loses control, and so would your nonprofit.

Lakeview Scaling

Lakeview has a priority that is not unusual among churches: Church planting. The idea, of course is to grow more churches. There are a variety of ways to do this, and Lakeview has chosen to help people grow their own churches in other communities (from coast to coast in the United States as well as overseas) with financial and volunteer support until the new church is up and running on its own. Lakeview has no control or influence over the local church's plans, budgets, or decisions.

Other churches have a different model, that of satellite sites. McLean Bible Church, in Tyson's Corner, Virginia, uses this model. McLean has a number of satellites (called campuses) in locations all over the Washington, D.C., metro area. Parishioners come to a campus, are greeted by local staff (employees of McLean) and hear a live praise band. At the appointed hour all the satellites get a live streaming video feed of the sermon for the week. Each satellite organizes its own small group bible studies, its own community outreach, and so on, but the home church keeps significant control over the campuses.

To recap, the core decision you have to make is about control. The model you choose will, in large part, be driven by how much control you and your board feel you need to be successful in scaling. After that decision is made, your options will become much clearer.

Going to Scale—A Checklist

As readers of all my books know, I love checklists. Really, that's what the Smart Stewardship decision tree is all about. In this case, though, I'm going to provide you with a more standard checklist to use if and when you decide to go to scale:

☐ What model or models of service are we going to scale up?
  ■ You may decide to scale your entire operation in another location, or just certain services. This is the point to figure that out.

- [ ] What will we lead with, culture or process?
  - In large part, a decision to go with culture will almost certainly lead to a need for more control over the new locations (see the next question).
- [ ] How much control do we feel we need to insure high-quality services are being delivered?
  - More control, more cost. Less control, less assurance that things will be done your way.
- [ ] Have we done a full feasibility study and business plan for our scaling?
  - No excuses, do a full feasibility study and if the numbers run, a full business plan. Scaling is a huge move. Do the necessary planning, and get outside help if you need it.
- [ ] Are our funders and community on board with our decision?
  - Don't blindside your best friends. Let them know the mission reason and how it will affect the services they currently fund or are attached to.
- [ ] Have we involved all employees and volunteers in this decision in some manner?
  - More neurons on the problem means better ideas and more owner- ship. Do it.

Answer all these questions thoroughly, refer back to our Smart Steward- ship decision tree, and you'll avoid the most common traps in scaling. Fi- nally, I would strongly recommend that you talk to other nonprofits that have scaled up. Talk to them about control, cash, quality, all the things I've raised with you in this chapter and in the rest of the book. Learn from their experiences, good and bad.

Going to scale may be a great option for you. Or not. Or not right now. The most important thing is that the decision to scale be your decision, not one you're forced into. Now you have the tools to make that decision and move your mission forward.

Recap

In this chapter, we've looked at the option of mission growth on steroids: Going to scale. Scaling is not a decision to be taken lightly, and we exam- ined the benefits and drawbacks in detail. I gave you my definition of "going to scale" which is *"Institutionalizing programs in a way that allows you to reach more of a target audience, usually in a larger geographic area."*

We started at the beginning with the often-overlooked issue of whether or not your key service or methods of provision can be duplicated. I showed you that to scale you need to have an idea or service that can be replicated without you on site. More importantly, we discussed the need to decide whether you are going to try to export a process or your culture first, and looked at some examples.

Then we turned to the truth about models and I urged you to remember that models are not cut and paste. Replicating a model successfully is dependent on both the community where it's being implemented and on the champion—the leader—on-site. Again, we looked at some examples.

I examined the idea of a reasonable growth curve may be for you, suggested that you pace your growth—with slow and steady being interrupted with intervals of faster growth, since you can run out of quality, cash, and capacity very, very fast if you grow too quickly. And, in a related issue, we examined the question of how much time, talent, and treasure you want to invest in your scaling efforts, and I showed you some ripple effects of those investments.

We turned to the key question in marketing, one often ignored by nonprofits intent on doing more mission: Does the market really want what you have to offer? It sounds so obvious, but in the quest to meet a need, we often forget that people will see what they want. Thus you need to ask, ask often, and really listen to the answers people give you.

Once these questions were resolved, we turned to the various ways people scale, and looked at many different examples. I told you that the first question you have to resolve is how much control you want. That's the strategic starting point. After you resolve that issue, the choices on the ground can be described as follows, in decreasing order of control:

- Open more offices
- Establish one or more subsidiaries
- Brand and methodology copyrighting
- Open source

Finally, I gave you a checklist to go through before going to scale. The checklist was:

- ☐ What model or models of service are we going to scale up?
- ☐ What will we lead with, culture or process?
- ☐ How much control do we feel we need to insure high-quality services are being delivered?
- ☐ Have we done a full feasibility study and business plan for our scaling?
- ☐ Are our funders and community on board with our decision?
- ☐ Have we involved all employees and volunteers in this decision in a significant way?

Scaling is a huge mission opportunity as well as a huge risk for your organization. It can help more people in more places, spread your brand, diversify your income stream, stretch your organization in both good and bad ways. It can also empty your bank account, stress your staff and board, and reduce your focus on your current community. In short, it's a big, big decision.

But, most importantly, going to scale needs to be *your* choice, a Smart Stewardship decision made by your staff and board, and not because you are urged to (or strong armed) by a funder. Your organization. Your choice.

When we talk about growing, we're primarily talking about good, optimistic, smiley-face things: Doing more mission, spreading our good works. And our Smart Stewardship decision tree can help us make the best decision possible. But what about the reverse? What if we've come upon bad times, as so many nonprofits have in the past few years? What then? How are we Smart Stewards in difficult times? That's the subject of our next chapter.

Discussion Questions

1. After reading this chapter, do we want to grow quickly? Do we think we can go to scale? Why or why not?
2. What would the mission benefits be? Could we grow rapidly and hang on to our core values?
3. If we grow, should we focus on replicating process or replicating culture?
4. What's a reasonable growth rate for us? How do we approach that issue strategically?
5. What models are appealing to us? How much control are we willing to give up?
6. What other organizations that we're familiar with can we talk to about rapid growth?

CHAPTER 9

Smart Stewardship in Difficult Times

Chapter Thumbnail

Overview

This book has shown you how to make better decisions, how to be a Smart Steward, and thus how to maximize your nonprofit's mission-effectiveness. The Smart Stewardship Decision tree and its components can guide you, helping you, your staff, and board make the good choices your community expects and, in fact, depends on.

Many of the examples you've seen have had to do with growth or expansion situations, because the strongest nonprofits are often in situations where growing their mission is an option, whether it be slow organic growth or going to scale. These nonprofits may choose to grow or chose to stay the same size, but they have the choice.

Weaker organizations are often caught in survival mode, making decisions to help get them through the next week, next quarter, next fiscal year, but never being able to look beyond. Not the best way to run an organization, but the reality for many nonprofits.

But strong or weak, crises come to all of us. Murphy's Law rears up, or as the ubiquitous bumper sticker (sort of) says: "Stuff Happens." A funder backs away, a government budget gets cut, a change in policy results in less of what you do being at the center of things. Frantic meetings (of board and staff) and much angst ensues. Staff are stressed, board members are stressed, the people you serve may even be stressed. It's not fun.

If you've had something like this occur to your organization, you know what I'm talking about. And, trust me, if this hasn't happened to your non-profit, it will. In this chapter we'll talk about how to be a Smart Steward when times are tough. Sometimes, the hardest thing to do when there's a crisis is figure out where to start: I'll show you. Then, we'll talk about strategic questions to ask, as well as tactical ones, and I'll provide you with some very hands-on things you can do.

Speaking of you, your organization is much more likely to come out of the crisis well if you lead well, and I'll give you a leadership checklist to check back with often during the crisis to make sure you have not abandoned your Smart Stewardship skills in all the chaos and stress.

And crises can be both chaotic and stressful. But they also are the most important tests of our stewardship skills, of our values, and of our commitment to our organization's mission. You want to get it right the first time: A ton of people are depending on you, so let's get to it.

In a Crisis, Start Here

Let's set the scene: Your largest funder (90 percent of your overall budget) has just called and told you that next fiscal year (beginning in 60 days) their funding of you is going to be cut between 10 percent and 15 percent across the board. They'll know better (will it be 10 or 15?) within a month. This follows last week's news that your largest donor, a local bank, has been bought by a huge national bank, and their annual donation of more than 5 percent of your total income is on hold as the merger is sorted out. Thus, you may lose between 10 and 20 percent of your total funding starting in two months.

Demand is up for your services, due to the recession. Your staff have not gotten raises in two years. Your accreditation review is coming up in six months and you need to focus staff on that, even though it's expensive in both time and money.

Your organization has the equivalent of 45 days of cash in the bank, but you also have a large mortgage on your building.

You hang up the phone with your funder and all this goes through your mind. What are you, what is your organization going to do? How can you get through this? There are so many unknowns! Will it be a 10 percent cut (difficult, but not catastrophic) or 20 percent (we'd *have* to cut services significantly and lay off staff!). Are any cuts one time, or just the beginning of further cuts? Is it just us, or are other organizations like ours getting hit? Can we re-focus on other funders to make up the difference? What am I going to tell my staff? My board?

At this moment, most leaders jump up and need to do *something*. They may need to take a walk, call a colleague for advice, touch in with home, call their board president, or convene a staff meeting. But they, you, we almost always need to be in motion. And this is the first trap of a crisis.

We're the leaders. Did you ever think about how or why we got to *be* the leaders? Did we get our jobs because we're good looking, or funny or smart? While we might like to think so, we really got to our positions of leadership because we could successfully solve problems. We could figure out how to make the service needs of our community match up with our budget. We could figure out how to make that reluctant donor or volunteer get involved with our mission. We could solve many problems big and small, and were thus noticed, promoted, and wound up where we are now. What we didn't do was sit there and let others work. We jumped in and fixed stuff. We did *something*.

And that's our tendency in a crisis, to immediately do *something*. Pick one small thing and do it and do it now and get started and fix the problem and save the mission and not lay anyone off and show the community we're still here and . . . .

And thus the trap: The first thing we need to do is stop and think.

 FOR EXAMPLE: I told you earlier that in college I was a paramedic in an emergency room, and later as a VISTA Volunteer. I rode ambulances a lot as well. First as an EMT and later as a paramedic you are told over and over when arriving on a scene NOT to simply grab someone, NOT to jump right in but to take a second or two (and just that) to "Stop. Breathe. Think. Do." It's easy, for example, to run up to someone who is lying on the ground check their pulse . . . and electrocute yourself because you didn't look at the electric wire that they are still touching that caused their heart attack. It's easy to put pressure on a wound, but not take the time to see if it's caused by a compound fracture . . . and thus you're doing more harm than good by pushing down without thinking the situation through. You have to react and, in many cases, you have to act *quickly*, but if you act *rashly*, if you just do *something*, you can hurt the patient more than you help. ■

So it is with our organizations in crisis. We can do more harm than good if we don't think things through. If you call an all-staff meeting now (just because you need to do something) what will you tell them? A 10 percent cut? 15 percent? Maybe 20 percent? What good will that do now? If you call your board president right now, what will you tell her?

Stop. Breathe. Think.

Okay, fine, you say. What do you want me to think about? Since you don't want me to talk to anyone, what do I do?

Actually, I *do* want you to talk to people, and lots of them. I just don't want you to do it rashly. I want you, the leader, to start the thought process that you will (very quickly) expand to senior staff, board, more staff, and volunteers and others.

I want you to think first about your mission. If you want something useful to do right now, get your mission statement out and read it. Slowly. Aloud. I know this sounds dopey: Just do it. Listen to your own voice. Why is your organization there? Who do your serve? Keep in mind that the mission is the reason, the mission is the point.

Then, take out a piece of paper and write, in large letters, your list of values. As you deal with the crisis, you need to look at that list at the beginning, middle, and end of every day, making sure that you are not violating your values, taking values shortcuts, due to your current hard times. Again, this may sound trite, just do it.

Now, you've done *something*. In fact, two things. Two important Smart Stewardship things. And *now* you can get on with the crisis, because you've set your framework.

And, I suggest you start by asking the questions that follow, which will give you both more information, and get your board and staff focused on the issue in a productive manner. They, too, will want to do something, and these questions will get them going.

NOTE: While my scenario above has to do with funding cuts (far, far too common in the nonprofit sector) a crisis could also take shape in terms of a legal or ethical issue that's wound up in the paper, an unexpected loss of accreditation, or some other unforeseen major impact on your program. As we work through the questions below, you'll see I've played out the funding-cut scenario above, but you can substitute any crisis in here and the sequence you use is the same.

Starting Questions

These questions are a combination of strategic and information gathering, and get you started on dealing with your problem/crisis. Some of these questions can be answered relatively quickly, some will take some time and investigation. It's almost always better to include more people in the discussion.

How Bad Is the Shortfall, Really?   Rumors are deadly in a crisis, as we'll see when we discuss internal and external communications. But they can hurt you here as well. In our scenario, when you hang up from the call with your funder you need to do some quick investigation. Is what you've been told by your funder (particularly if it's a government funder) final or just precautionary? When does the cut go into effect? Is it for one program or all programs from that funder? Is anything specifically included or excluded?

 HANDS ON: If the potential funding cut is from a government agency, make sure to check both with other organizations like yours who get funding from the same entity as well as from your state or federal trade association. Is this much ado about nothing or a serious issue? ■

The task at this point is to find out how bad things *really* are, for how long, and for what reason. The next two questions will also help establish the true situation.

What's the Cause of the Shortfall? Is the funding being cut because of a change of policy or legislation or is funding being cut because your organization lost its accreditation, or due to a political compromise that's still in the works.

 FOR EXAMPLE: My first chief executive (CEO) job was for a nonprofit that received 95 percent of its funds from the U.S. government under federal legislation. I'd had the CEO job less than two weeks when the first Reagan/Stockman budget came out. In the budget, our program was eliminated. One hundred percent gone, starting in six months. Ouch. I found out this great news from a call from my federal project officer who said "You're going to be shut down by the end of September. Sorry."

Since there were 230 similar organizations like mine around the country, I got on the phone to our national trade association who assured me that the first budget was nothing more than political posturing. They didn't say "don't worry, everything's fine." They told me to get on a plane to come to DC to lobby for the program. But they also said that they expected us to take a 10 to 15 percent cut over two years and to start planning for that.

I got on the plane (as did many other CEOs) and our cuts wound up being more like 20 percent over two years. But the point is that a) my federal program officer had incomplete information, and b) we weren't eliminated, not even close. It was, of course, a long-term cut, due to a seismic change in the political landscape, not just a one-time event. ■

Is This a One-Time or Systemic Problem?   Speaking of one-time, your next question is just that: Is this a one-time budget hole filler for the funder, or a result of what looks like long-term adjustments? If you have the cash, you can ride out a one-time cut, but if it looks like its systemic, you need to start thinking about ramping down to some level.

FOR EXAMPLE: In the early 1990s, the state of Illinois came up with an innovative way to balance its books for the fiscal year. Rather than coming to a political compromise, it simply didn't pay the non-profits it funded for services like home care, residential placements for people with chronic mental health, foster care, and the like for the first 60 days of the fiscal year.

The nonprofits got a letter on July 1 (the first day of the fiscal year) stating that their payments would be held for 60 days. For many organizations, including one on whose board I served, this was a cash crisis of the highest order: they were 90 to 100 percent state funded. How were they going to pay salaries, rent, insurance, and the like for nearly one quarter of the year?

It was hard, very hard, but the good news was that the cut wasn't to the *budget*, it was to *cash*. All the agencies were going get their full funds eventually, just that there was going to be a 60 day delay. It was a one-time (or so we thought) problem.   ■

So, again, ask around, talk to as many people as possible. Get more neurons on the issue.

HANDS ON: This kind of analysis is essential before you do anything else, including sending a formal update to your board or bringing your staff up to speed. You need to get as close to the truth as you can before you either upset people unduly or give them an all clear when it's anything but.   ■

At this point, you have analyzed the true nature of the problem, as best you can. Now come some big, big questions.

Is Organizational Viability at Risk?   Let's start with the worst case. With this cut as you now understand it, will you potentially lose the organization? If you have no cash cushion, or if the cut will devastate your core mission, the continuation of the organization may well be in question. There are two parts to this question. The first is, of course, financial. Will we be able to support our organization without this funding?

FOR EXAMPLE: In our scenario, we're only losing potentially 20 percent of your funding right? But what if that 20 percent throws off the profits that sustain two or three other programs? Or if that particular funding was matched? Sometimes cuts can cost more than just the money on the surface. ■

Your second question has to do with mission. Will the cuts cost you the program that is central to your mission, one that your other programs can't do without? For example, if a residential school for children with a particular disability loses substantial funding for its residences and the children can't live on campus, the school won't be able to fill its classrooms.

An ancillary question has to do, of course, with quality. Can you sustain adequate mission quality with these cuts?

The answer to the financial side of this question may cause you to *have* to close your organization. The answer to the mission side of this question may cause you to *choose* to close your organization.

Neither, of course are desirable in any way, but you have to check this out first. You may have to answer the next questions simultaneously, but you need to focus most on organizational viability.

Are Individual Services at Risk?

If the organization can survive, will all the services? Of course, an elimination of certain services may cause you to go back and look at organizational viability. Even if you don't have to shut the organization, you may have to stop doing one or more programs, either for money or for mission reasons. You need to look at a landscape without that program and ask: What else spills out if we cut this program? Do we lose needed administrative support? Do we lose our accreditation? Is this a core reason other donors or funders support us? Is it central to our board or volunteers? Can we do the program on 10, 15, or 20 percent less money? What would that look like?

Are Legal Responsibilities/Contractual Services at Risk?

Even if your organization can weather the cuts and even if you won't have to cut an entire program you still have one more review to do: your contracts. Will your planned accommodation to the funding cuts result in violation of some other contract or obligation?

 FOR EXAMPLE: If you plan to reduce space, will you violate your lease? If you plan to move staff around, will you be in violation of another funder contract that calls for X Full Time Equivalents (FTEs) on *their* contract? Are you using any of the funding for match on other contracts? The answers to these questions and others will only come from a review of all your contracts. ■

HANDS ON: Don't do this review by yourself. Have a group read through all your obligation documents, even if you think you know them by heart. You may well be surprised at what you find, and if so, you want to find it now, not later. ■

Once you've finished this analysis, you're ready to really jump in to the next phase, and are armed to talk to your board and staff with a true analysis of the situation.

As we've already discussed, your tendency next will be to jump into fixing things, and those will almost certainly be small things, things I call tactical problems. You don't want to start there. You, your staff, and board need to take the time to deal with strategy first. Yes, even in a crisis, actually more so in a crisis, you need to take a bit of time to think strategically, think long.

FOR EXAMPLE: If you've ever had the fun of being in a canoe on a quiet lake, you know the joy of just moseying along. If you're sitting in the stern you can look at and talk to the person in the bow, look around the canoe at the water, notice what's going on, perhaps dip your hand in the lake. You can take the short views, because the water is calm.

But when the wind comes up, the storm comes, you have to take the long view. To get to the far shore, you can't just look at the back of the person in the bow of your canoe. You have to pick a spot on the far shore and head the boat to that spot: You have to look farther ahead. ■

You're in a storm now, and you need to stop, breathe, think—and think strategically first, then tactically. And that's the sequence of actions I'm going to give you, strategic ones first, then tactical.

Strategic Issues/Actions

As you begin to look at your strategy around your crisis, you won't be too surprised where I start. Some of the issues/actions below were covered in our Starting Questions earlier, but merit, for different reasons, another look, because this time you'll be doing the looking, discussing, and deciding in a group.

HANDS ON: You're ready now to convene a crisis team. The composition of your team will depend, of course, on your organization and the situation, but you want senior staff and a few key board members on the team, as well as outside advisors if necessary. For example, you may want your attorney, or your banker, or a former board member, if they have certain skills and/or perspectives helpful in the current crisis.

Start by giving them the current situation based on your earlier research. Give them a sequence of events that led up to the crisis, their charge as a group, and the time frame they have to make their decisions and/or plans.

Urge them to keep the discussions confidential, particularly if potential layoffs are on the table in any way, shape, or form. Again, the rumor mill is a deadly enemy. ■

After all of that, go through the following steps:

■ Review your mission and values statement.

Hand out the mission and values, and have someone read it aloud. Tell everyone that this is the key framework you want to work within, and violating any of the values would seriously damage the organization. Also, what does your mission tell you about your priorities? Does it highlight one demography or location over another?

■ Review your strategic plan.

Assuming you have a strategic plan, what does it tell you about your priorities? Are there areas noted in the plan that are your core competencies, or the focus of your attention? You spent considerable time and money putting your strategic plan together. Use that investment now.

■ Review your marketing plan.

After looking carefully at your strategic plan, drill down a bit by looking at your marketing plan. That document, again the result of a lot of good and careful thought, should tell you which of your markets are your target ones, and which are less crucial. You can also review any asking you had done prior to writing your marketing plan to see if there are any insights you can glean. Why do you want to know your target markets? Because if you have to cut services, you want to attempt to cut services that serve those targets as late as possible, if not last.

■ Talk (again) to peer organizations.

I know you had discussions with your peers when we talked about starting questions earlier, but now is a great opportunity to do it again. Time has passed, you know more about your situation, and you and your peers have all had time to come up with some solutions to the cuts. Talking to your peer organizations is one of many ways to put more neurons on the problem.

■ Talk (again) to your state/national trade association.

Same thing here. You talked to your trade groups earlier, but with the passage of time, everyone has learned more, adapted more, come up with ways to accommodate. Most importantly, the state or national trade group should have up-to-the minute information on whether cuts (again, only for government funding) are going to be as severe as predicted, start when forecast, and so on.

■ Is there a need for long-term strategic restructuring such as a merger or partnering?

This is one of the biggest issues you'll face. Another way to put it is this: Is your business model still viable given the cuts you're facing? Do you have to rethink the core way you fund, operate, staff, and maintain your quality level?

One of the choices in this area is not just restructuring internally, but contracting out some of your services (including administrative tasks like payroll or all human resources), or partnering with another nonprofit (sharing revenue but also expense) or, in rare cases, a full merger of two organizations to provide some economies of scale.

 HANDS ON: Be fully aware that the partnership/merger option almost always results in a reduction of staff. If your nonprofit is like most others, 70 to 90 percent of your expenses are personnel related. To cut costs, you have to cut people. Sad, hard, but true. ■

These strategic questions will focus you first on the biggest, most crucial issues, ones that can make sure you re-shape your organization or at least adjust to your crisis in the most mission-based manner.

Remember, too, the primary result of all your crisis-based decisions should be the four mission outcomes . . . more mission, better mission, more efficient mission, more effective mission. "*More* mission?" you say . . . how does that work in a 20 percent cut situation? It doesn't, obviously, but your crisis may well be the impetus to make your mission provision more efficient or more effective, which could result in less mission cuts per lost dollar than you originally anticipated.

Remember, too, that as you begin your review of the strategic issues, one resource for you is the Smart Stewardship decision tree, particularly if you are considering making major organizational changes.

Once you're through the strategy questions and have had significant group discussions about the impact of your situation, you're ready to move to the tactical side of things.

Tactical Issues/Actions

If strategy is the view from 30,000 feet, tactics is all about what's going on on the ground. There are a bunch of great things you can do in a crisis, but it's most important to remember to talk to the tactics experts—your front-line managers and the people who actually provide service. As you think through your crisis responses, add their neurons into the information gathering and decision making.

- Run *weekly* cash-flow projections.

    I've already urged you to do cash-flow projections for six months out. In non-crisis times, these cash flows can be month by month, or by payroll (perhaps twice a month, or every other Friday). But in a crisis, particularly one that cuts income, you have to rework your cash flows to show weekly receipts and disbursements. You still want to project out six full months, just at a more detailed level, and this level of detail allows you to really keep a handle on your cash status and how it will be changing down the road. Remember, cash equals oxygen. Don't run out of either cash or air in a crisis.

- Develop best-case, middle-case, and worst-case scenarios.

    Just as if you're going to scale, in a crisis you need business-planning skills. Here, your staff (perhaps bolstered by a talented board member) look at three scenarios: best-case, worst-case, and a middle-case. You should base your best, worst, middle on group decisions about what you've learned. Thus, in our scenario, the best case might be a 10 percent, two-year cut across the board, the worst case a 20 percent permanent cut, and the middle case a 15 percent cut.

    Now, run the cases out in time a bit. When do you need to reduce staff and by how much? What about services? Will you be able to hold on to your current space, or is it inevitable that you give it up?

 HANDS ON: As you develop your cases make sure you clearly list your assumptions so that you can adjust the outcomes as you learn more. This kind of effort is, by the way, what electronic spreadsheets were designed for, so use them to the max. It will make your job much, much easier. ■

This type of scenario building allows you to see what your options are. If, for example, you find that in the *best* case you have to let three staff go, and in the worst case it moves up to six layoffs, you are more likely to get started with the layoffs soon, something almost all of us put off.

 HANDS ON: Have trigger points in your scenarios as well. "If we don't get the foundation grant by *X* date, we lay three people off," or "When we run our reserves down to 45 days cash, that triggers four layoffs." ■

Obviously, these triggers do not always have to result in staff leaving; they could also result in a special board meeting, or abandoning a service. Whatever, it's my experience in working with dozens of nonprofits in financial crises that if you don't have the triggers in writing, you won't take the actions.

Finally with scenarios, you'll be using spreadsheets to run the numbers—make sure you run them on a cash basis, not accrual. Cash is what matters in a crisis.

Inform Staff and Board Early and Often

As you develop your information and scenarios, you'll be asked by staff, as well as board members between meetings, what's going on? Be available, be informative, be up front, but. . . .

Other than the people on your crisis team, only tell people *what you know*. Not what you *think* may happen, not what you *hope*, not what you *fear*. Only *what you know*. I cannot overemphasize the importance of this small, simple suggestion, nor warn you too much about how hard it is to stick to.

As the icon of your organization, people will look to you for leadership, of course, but also listen to every word you say, watch your body language and mood, even gossip about the meaning of what you wear ("Is that a happy blouse or an unhappy blouse?").

 FOR EXAMPLE: Let's look at our scenario. You've gotten word of 10 to 20 percent cuts and you go meet with staff to tell them what's going on. You note that at the current time, the best information you have says 10 to 20 percent cuts. That, you know. You tell the staff you've formed a crisis team to work the problem. That you also know. You tell them the crisis team, board, staff, and volunteers are going to work hard to minimize any negative impact on the mission. You know that, too.

"Boss," asks one staff person. "It seems to me we'll have to cut staff if the funding reductions are that big. Do you agree?"

Your appropriate response is, "I don't know about that. The crisis group will be looking at our situation. When I know more I'll tell you."

If you were instead to say something like "I hope not," or "I guess so," or "Layoffs are inevitable," you've just destroyed morale in the organization unnecessarily. Remember, you don't *know* yet. ■

HANDS ON: Your ability to have staff satisfied with your answer above will depend in huge part on their trust of you. If they hear you say "When I know more I'll tell you," do they say "blah, blah, blah," or "Okay, I believe her"? This goes back to being a leader who means what she says and says what she means, who leads with the organizational values and admits her mistakes. All that good stuff we talked about earlier in the book. ■

■ Review (again) your contractual obligations.

Make a second pass over your contracts, now that you have started to focus on your correction plan. Will any of your actions violate a current contract? If so, can you get the contract changed now? Remember to read your leases and your loan agreements, as well as all your funding contracts. Have more than one person do this review. Don't trust just one set of eyes.

■ Check state and federal labor laws and collective bargaining agreements.

For most nonprofits, anything other than a minor funding cut will result in a reduction in force: less staff. Sometimes this can be accomplished by not filling a slot of someone who leaves voluntarily. That's great when it happens, but the situation is rare. Most of the time, layoffs ensue. So, now's the time to review state and federal laws as well as any collective bargaining agreements you may have for limitations and guidelines.

■ If layoffs are necessary, do them carefully, soon, and in a value-laden manner.

Let's be up front: Laying off an employee who did nothing wrong is awful. It's hard, it's emotional, and it's not fair. All of us who've done it shudder to think about ever doing it again.

And that's the reason this item is so important. Remember our discussion about values-laden layoffs in Chapter 4? There, I showed you a 2×2 layoff grid where one axis was labeled Legal and Illegal, and the other was labeled Right and Wrong. You need to do your layoffs in a totally legal manner, of course, but also in the *right* way—according to your values. People will remember how you laid off their peers as much as the fact that you did.

Secondly, do it sooner rather than later. Use your scenario triggers to help get you going. In almost every financial crisis I've worked with, managers hold on to their staff too long. It's understandable, it's very human, but it's not very humane. Nor is it smart stewardship: If the best-case scenario you've developed says you'll have to let four people go, why are you waiting?

Sooner, legal, and values laden.

Communicate, Communicate, and Communicate

As your crisis team comes up with solutions and plans, communicate both internally and externally. This doesn't mean just sitting in your office and sending out emails. Get out of your office and meet with your employees and volunteers informally. Tell them what you know, of course, but also just be visible. You're communicating more than just words when people see you.

Use your web site, Facebook, Twitter, and other communications media to update people about your status and its impact on your mission. Let them know you're aggressively working to preserve your mission output.

Meet in person with key stakeholders, including your largest vendors, and any creditors you have. These people will be impressed you're working on your problem. Some CEOs have told me they avoided talking to vendors since they couldn't pay their entire bill, but were amazed when they did talk to the vendor to find that the vendor would much rather get a partial payment along with a plan of payments rather than nothing. Sounds pretty obvious when I put it that way, doesn't it? Talk to people once you have your plan in place. Tell them what you know, and focus your conversations around your mission.

Prepare for the Media

The larger your organization, the more people you serve, or the more people you are letting go, the more likely it is that the media will call. Be prepared by assigning all media inquiries to one person, and make sure that person has some training in how to deal with the press.

Have you ever noticed how much more often you see a "Spokesperson for_____" being quoted in a story rather than a celebrity, CEO, or executive director? There's a reason for that; the trained spokesperson is much more likely to give a consistent, non-harmful answer.

 HANDS ON: Want to develop the shortest policy you've ever heard of? Here's your new Media Policy.

"When contacted by the press or outside news organizations for comment, all inquiries are to be directed to (<u>NAME</u>). No one else is to comment on behalf of the agency."

That's it.

Now, make sure that all your board and staff play by this rule. By the way, if your crisis is a legal or moral one (i.e., someone associated with your organization has been accused of something illegal or immoral) you have to have to—*have to*—live by this policy. ∎

These tactical actions will keep you moving in the direction of the best possible solution to your crisis. But the strategic and tactical parts of our crisis management operation are not all we have to pay attention to. We also have to make sure we're leading in the best way possible.

Leadership Issues

In a crisis, leadership is critical. You have to lead from the front, you have to be visible, you have to do so many things well that you'll feel pressure to be perfect. Get over it, you aren't. But you can use the checklist below to remind yourself of the most important things you need to attend to. The first one may surprise you!

Am I Taking Care of the Leader?

I know most CEOs would put this last. "Take care of me? I'm the least important thing I have to worry about." Wrong. You're the leader and in a crisis more people are depending on you in more ways than ever.

One of the biggest challenges leaders face in a crisis is not getting sick, not being so tired that they make bad decisions, not getting critically ill. So you need to take care of yourself and this needs to be intentional, not merely "when there's time."

 HANDS ON: Eat three meals a day, and not just wolfing down food on the run. Stop. Sit. Eat, and don't eat alone at your desk.

Sleep at least seven hours a night. If you're so stressed you can't sleep, lie in the dark and at least rest your body and your eyes. You'll need them.

Continue some regimen of exercise. You may have to cut back those long runs, or three-times-a-week weight workouts, or reduce yoga to once a week, but don't eliminate it. If your body is used to the exercise it will feel much worse if you stop—and so will your head.

"Get away" for at least 30 minutes during the day. Take a walk, close your office door and take a quick nap, stretch, meditate, whatever works, but take the break. ■

The stress on you is relentless, lonely, and huge. Take care of the leader.

Am I Putting Mission First?

In working with lots of CEOs and boards during their financial crises, I've repeatedly heard this goal. "My top goal is that I want to get through this crisis without layoffs." My response is always . . . "Why?"

When they look at me like I'm mad, I follow up, "Is your mission to employ your staff? No, it's to help in the area of (whatever their mission is). Your primary goal should be to do the best mission possible." The CEOs and boards don't like it when I say that, but they (usually) grudgingly agree: Mission first.

As the leader in your nonprofit's crisis, it is crucial that you lead with mission, talk about mission, discuss decisions in light of mission. You'll show everyone the way, and by doing so keep mission front and center even when you're not in the room.

Remember these two challenges: Am I more concerned about the organization or the people we serve? Am I more concerned about the staff or the people we serve?

Tough questions, but you're in tough times.

Am I Leading Our Values from the Front?

Again, as leader, you're always on. People will listen to what you say, watch what you do, analyze your body language. Everyone in the organization will be on edge and if your actions, words, or even body language violate your values, you will damage all the values work you've done.

Happily, your values work also gives you a common format going forward. When you tell staff that the crisis team has decided to (do whatever it decides) and you note how the decision was made in accord with your values, people will understand. They may not agree, but you'll at least start on the same page.

Am I Asking the Hard Questions?

My father had a favorite saying, one that he lived by. "If you have a set of tasks to accomplish and it doesn't matter which comes first, always pick the hardest one to start with." I try (with some success, but not enough) to live up to that standard. Picking the hard (long, tedious, or uncomfortable) thing first makes everything that comes after seem so easy.

In a crisis, everything seems hard. But even in this hardscape, it's easy to not face up to the hardest, most difficult questions, and as a leader you need to ask them, ask them early, and ask them regularly. Questions like these:

- Can our organization *really* survive this crisis in a condition where we can provide mission we're proud of?
- Can we get through this without cutting services, or should we pare back a complete service or part of two or three?
- Who am I going to lay off?
- Do I need to change the management team to accommodate our new needs?

- Do I need to change the board to improve our governance skillset?
- Is the crisis something I should have seen coming? Do I need to change the way I do my job?

None of these questions (and dozens of others like them) are easy, but they should be rattling around in your head, and you should pose them, if no one else does, with your crisis team.

Do I Have All the Information I Can Get?

This item should remind you to ask more, listen better, and widen your net for possible solutions. Put more neurons on the problem, and also research (with peer organizations, trade associations, etc.) what solutions are out there.

 HANDS ON: If you're like most of us in a crisis you never have *all* the information you want, so don't fall victim to using that lack of complete information to staff big decisions or put off the triggers in your scenarios. I've heard far too many leaders say "We'll just wait until Monday and then decide . . . we may get some new information . . . " and say that week after week after week. ■

Use your scenario triggers to move ahead.

Am I Sharing Information Widely?

People can't help you if they don't know what's going on. Share what you know as you know it. Whether in person or online, let people know what's going on and how they can help. Keeping people in the dark will just make them more concerned and rev up the rumor mill.

Remember what John Chambers, the CEO of Cisco says: "No one of us is as smart as all of us." That's true, but you can short-circuit that truth by not sharing information.

Am I Leading Optimistically?

One last time, as the leader, people look to you. I'm not suggesting you act like a Pollyanna, nor am I urging you to lie to your staff, and tell them everything is fine. But being positive, telling staff they're doing a great job, being frank and also positive is crucial. Listen to two statements that a CEO could make to a staff meeting during a crisis. Both are the same information. Which would make you happier to hear?

"Well, folks, we've got a big challenge ahead of us. Our budget's been cut and our funders are continuing to pound us. The people we serve are depending on us to be there and that's putting pressure on everyone. This is a hard time to be here, perhaps the hardest in my 20 years at this agency. I know some of you, like me, are losing sleep and I'm sorry. Hang in there, and we'll see how this goes."

or

"Well, people, interesting times. We've got huge challenges right now. You know our budget has been cut and that's going to require some changes, but the most important thing for us to remember is that the people we serve, those folks who depend on us, they're still there. As always, mission first.

This is hard for everyone, no question, and I wish I could tell you how it was all going to turn out. I can tell you that a lot of people are working the problem very hard right now, and that I need your help as well.

I can also tell you I'd rather be here, now, going through this with you than anywhere else. As long as we live by our values and pursue our mission, the rest will work itself out."

You set the tone. You set the attitude. If you act like Eeyore in the Winnie the Pooh stories, everyone else will act the same. Lead optimistically.

Crises are hard. And inevitable. And opportunities to make needed changes that have been put off. Crises can bring people together or drive them apart. In many ways, a crisis will test all the good Smart Stewardship work you've already done. Lead with the mission, live by the values, and you'll come through with your organization in the best shape possible.

Recap

In this chapter, we've examined what Smart Stewards need to do to lead their nonprofits successfully through a crisis. Whether you are a strong organization or a weak one, crises come to all, and crises present unique leadership challenges.

I started you at the beginning: Where to start in a crisis. I told you to Stop. Breathe. Think. And to fight the tendency that nearly all leaders have to jump in and do *something*, anything at the beginning of a crisis. I urged you to both read your mission aloud to yourself and write down your values as a starting point for your leadership in any crisis. I know it sounded dumb, but it sets some mental limits for you as a Smart Steward.

I gave you some starting questions, to get your board and staff moving and gather key information. These starting questions were:

- How bad is the shortfall, really?
- What's the cause of the shortfall?
- Is this a one-time or systemic problem?
- Is organizational viability at risk?
- Are individual services at risk?
- Are legal responsibilities/contractual services at risk?

Then we turned to the key questions of leading, starting with the strategic ones, not the tactical ones. This may sound counterintuitive—it's a crisis! We don't have time to sit around and dither about strategy! The problem, of course, is that a crisis can be compounded if you don't think through the strategic impacts of what's going on.

So, we started with strategy. To recap, the actions I suggested were:

- ☐ Review your mission and values statement
- ☐ Review your strategic plan
- ☐ Review your marketing plan
- ☐ Talk to peer organizations
- ☐ Talk to state/national trade associations
- ☐ Is there a need for long-term strategic restructuring?

After that, I gave you the more hands-on questions and actions you really wanted to get to, the tactical checklist. Again to recap, they were:

- ☐ Run weekly cash-flow projections
- ☐ Develop best-case, middle-case, and worst-case scenarios
- ☐ Inform staff and board early and often
- ☐ Review contractual obligations
- ☐ Check state labor laws and collective bargaining agreements
- ☐ If layoffs are necessary, do them carefully, soon, and value laden
- ☐ Communicate, communicate, and communicate
- ☐ Prepare for the media

Finally, we turned to a leadership checklist. Leading through a crisis is huge. Leading through a crisis is hugely stressful. The checklist I provided is designed to help you be the best Smart Steward possible for your organization. The items on the checklist were:

- ☐ Am I taking care of the leader?
- ☐ Am I putting mission first?

☐ Am I leading our values from the front?
☐ Am I asking the hard questions?
☐ Do I have all the information I can get?
☐ Am I sharing information widely?
☐ Am I leading optimistically?

Crisis is inevitable. Crisis is also, as everyone knows, opportunity, although it's hard to see that when you hang up with the funder cutting you 10 to 20 percent. And just because things are hard doesn't mean you get a break from being a Smart Steward: In fact, it's more important for you to make good decisions in a crisis than at other times.

We've come a long way in our examination of how to be a better steward, a Smart Steward, for your nonprofit. I've got a few more words to say in the next chapter, and then some resources to help you as you move your organization ahead.

Discussion Questions

1. One of the most common crises out there is a natural disaster. Are our disaster policies up to speed? What about a succession policy (in case of severe illness or sudden death)?
2. Let's walk through the last crisis we faced. Did we deal with strategy first, or tactics? How can we be better next time?
3. Are there questions we would add to Peter's list of starting questions?
4. How about the leadership questions? Do these make sense? Is it unreasonable to take care of ourselves in a crisis?
5. How can we use our technology to better communicate with staff, board, and the community the next time we have a crisis?

CHAPTER 10

Final Words

If you've read this book, you care deeply about one or more nonprofits. You want to make sure that the mission those nonprofits produce is the best possible for the people they serve. Good for you.

As I said early on, whether you are a staff member, board member, non-governing volunteer, or a key funder, you're a steward of your nonprofit and the community resources that support it. Hopefully, by reading this book, you've improved your ability to make the best, smartest decisions on the strategic, tactical, and day-to-day levels to move your mission forward.

I probably misnamed this book: If you're like most readers you were already a "smart" steward when you opened the front cover. Now, though, it is my fondest hope that you are even smarter, even more capable, and that in being so, you see new possibilities for your organization.

Many millions of people around the world depend on nonprofits for everything from feeding their children to inspiring their spirit, for assistance with shelter for the night, or education to last a lifetime. Nonprofits touch every part of our lives every day. We are, truly, the glue that holds our society together.

Those of us who have chosen to work in the nonprofit sector have chosen a career of work for the betterment of others' lives, and there is no richer, more meaningful calling. As you move your organization forward, you'll have many decisions and choices to make. You now have the tools to make them in a more mission-enabling way.

Keep your mission front and center. Good luck on your journey.

Tools and Resources

The day I finished this appendix, in the early fall of 2011, a quick Google search for the search string "nonprofit decision-making" came up with thousands of articles, books, blog postings, and comments. No, I didn't read all 12,000 of them, but the point is that you've got many more resources than you can use.

What I've done here is to give you just a few of what I consider the best resources for you on better nonprofit decision making. Just a few great books, a few amazingly helpful papers, a couple of great blogs to subscribe to. I don't want you to bury yourself, but I do want you to be able to go beyond just what's covered in this book.

On the last page, you'll also see a list of my other books, all of which are designed to help you make your organization more mission capable.

Books

Small Giants: Companies That Choose to Be Great Instead of Big, by Bo Burlingham. New York: Portfolio Trade, 2007, ISBN 978-1591841494.

The Wisdom of Crowds, by James Surowiecki. New York: Anchor, 2005, ISBN 978-0385721707.

The Three Signs of a Miserable Job; a Fable for Managers (And Their Employees), by Pat Lencioni. San Francisco: Jossey-Bass, 2007, ISBN 978-0787995317.

Nonprofit Sustainability: Making Strategic Decisions for Economic Viability, by Jeanne Bell et al. San Francisco: Jossey-Bass, 2010, ISBN 978-0470598290.

The Nonprofit Organizational Culture Guide: Revealing the Hidden Truths That Impact Performance, by Paige Hull Teegarden, Denice Rothman Hinden, and Paul Sturm. San Francisco: Jossey-Bass, 2010, ISBN 978-0470891544.

Papers

"*The Nonprofit Starvation Cycle,*" by Ann Goggins Gregory and Don Howard. *The Stanford Social Innovation Review,* Fall, 2009.

"*RAPID Decision Making, What It Is, Why We Like It, and How to Get the Most Out of It,*"by Jon Huggett and Caitrin Moran. Bridgespan.org, 2007.

Web Resources

Peter Brinckerhoff's Web site, Mission-Based Management, with links to his blog:

http://missionbased.com

Kivi Leroux Miller's Nonprofit Marketing Blog:

www.nonprofitmarketingguide.com/blog/

The Chronicle of Philanthropy Blog, Give and Take:

http://philanthropy.com/blogs/giveandtake/

Books by Peter Brinckerhoff

Mission-Based Management: Leading Your Nonprofit in the 21st Century, Third Edition. Hoboken: John Wiley & Sons, 2010, ISBN 9780470432075.

Mission-Based Marketing: Positioning Your Nonprofit in an Increasingly Competitive World, Third Edition. Hoboken: John Wiley & Sons, 2009, ISBN 9780471296935.

Generations: The Challenge of a Lifetime for Your Nonprofit. Minneapolis, MN: Turner Publishing, 2007, ISBN 9780940069558.

Nonprofit Stewardship: A Better Way to Lead Your Mission-Based Organization. Minneapolis, MN: Turner Publishing, 2004, ISBN 9780940069428.

Social Entrepreneurship: The Art of Mission-Based Venture Development. New York: John Wiley & Sons, 2000, ISBN 9780471362821.

Faith-Based Management: Leading Organizations Based on More Than Just Mission. New York: John Wiley & Sons, 1999, ISBN 9780471315445.

About the Author

PETER BRINCKERHOFF has spent his entire adult life working in, around, and for not-for-profits. He is dedicated to the concept that a not-for-profit organization is a mission-based business, in the business of doing its mission.

When Peter formed his firm, Corporate Alternatives, Inc., in 1982 it was the first consulting and training company in the United States dedicated exclusively to the management concerns of 501(c)(3) organizations.

A former VISTA Volunteer, Peter knows how not-for-profits work from his experience as a volunteer, his work as a staff member and later as executive director of two regional not-for-profits, and from his service on numerous state, local, and national not-for-profit boards. He brings this understanding of the many perspectives in a not-for-profit organization to his work.

Peter is an award-winning author, with eight books and two workbooks in print, and more than 60 articles published in the not-for-profit press. Three of his books, *Mission-Based Management, Financial Empowerment*, and his newest, *Generations, The Challenge of a Lifetime for Your Nonprofit*, each won the prestigious Terry McAdam Award from the Alliance for Nonprofit Management. The award is given for "The Best New Nonprofit Book" each year. He is the only author to win the award multiple times. Peter's books are used as texts in courses in undergraduate and graduate nonprofit management programs at more than 100 colleges and universities worldwide.

Peter is also a highly acclaimed speaker and lecturer, presenting his ideas on how to make not-for-profits more effective to dozens of audiences across North America, in Europe and Asia each year.

From 2003 to 2007, Peter was an Adjunct Professor of Nonprofit Management at the Kellogg School of Management at Northwestern University. He taught the core graduate course in the Nonprofit Management program at Kellogg. In addition, Peter has guest lectured at the graduate level at Boston University, University of Colorado, University of Illinois, and Vanderbilt University.

Peter received his Bachelor's Degree from the University of Pennsylvania, and his Master's Degree in Public Health Administration from Tulane University. Raised in Connecticut, Peter and his family lived in Springfield, Illinois, from 1977 to 2007. Peter and his wife now call Union Hall, Virginia, home.

Peter can be reached at peter@missionbased.com.

Index